PÉTER MUJZER

BARBAROSSA CAMPAIGN IN 1941

HUNGARIAN PERSPECTIVE

KAGERO

Acknowledgements
I would like to thank the following individuals and institutes for their kind support in terms of information and photographs, without which this book might not have been possible: Babucs Zoltán, Bonhardt Attila, Deák Tamás, Fortepan, HIM, Illésfalvi Pétet, Móker József, Mujzer Péter, Pálinkás Zsolt, War Correspondent Company.

First Edition

AUTHOR
Péter Mujzer

PHOTO CREDITS
Babucs Zoltán, Bonhardt Attila, Deák Tamás, Fortepan, HIM, Illésfalvi Pétet, Móker József, Mujzer Péter, Pálinkás Zsolt, War Correspondent Company

MAPS
– Over all map based on Ungváry Krisztián: A magyar honvédség a második világháborúban, Osiris Kiadó 2005,
– Tactical maps based on original maps published in the Hungarian Military Review from 1942-1944 and Csima János: Források a Magyar Honvédség II. világháborús történetének tanulmányozásához, Zrínyi Kiadó, 1961

COLOR PROFILES
Alessandro Cordasco, Camillo Cordasco, Arkadiusz Wróbel, Sławomir Zajączkowski, Deák Tamás

TRANSLATION/PROOFREADING
Péter Mujzer

DTP
KAGERO STUDIO - Łukasz Maj

LUBLIN 2021

ISBN 978-83-66673-67-0

KAGERO Publishing
Akacjowa 100, os. Borek, Turka
20-258 Lublin 62, Poland
phone/fax +48 81 501-21-05
e-mail: kagero@kagero.pl, marketing@kagero.pl, shop@kagero.pl
www.kagero.pl, shop.kagero.pl

Table of contents

Introduction

In this book, I would like to introduce to our readers the first major campaign of the Royal Hungarian Army fought against the Red Army in Ukraine from July until November of 1941. The book deals with the history of Hungary from the end of WW1 until 1941. Specially attention was given to the Hungarian Army between the wars, how it was organized, trained, equipped, and armed. The second part of the text focus on the military operation performed by the Carpathian Operational Group and the Mobile Corps in Ukraine, in 1941. A separate chapter contains the operational history of the Royal Hungarian Air Force during the campaign. The text is accompanied by original photographs, maps, and color profiles. The majority of the photos coming from the Fortepan collection added some extra photos from my collection.

The Hungarian Fortepan is a free-to-use, community photo archive where you can browse and download over a hundred thousand archive photos for free, in good quality. I do have the privilege and the opportunity to closely follow the work of the Fortepan, currently having almost 150000 photos from 1900 until 1989. A significant part of the collection contains photos about military-related topics. I widely use Fortepan to illustrate my articles and books. Reviewing the year of 1941 at Fortepan, I did recognize a huge number of unpublished and unknown photos covering the history of the Hungarian military operation in the former Polish and Ukrainian territories concerning the fighting during the Barbarossa Campaign from late June until early November 1941.

By that time, having a camera was an interest of few. Mostly reserve officers, skilled enlisted men, and some professional soldiers; officers and NCOs took their camera to capture their journey into the "Soviet Paradise", as it was ironically referred to by the propaganda. Most of the Fortepan photos belonged to some dedicated photographer; reserve ensign Pál Berkó served at the 151th Motorized Bridge Column, Károly Hajdú Fedő fought with the 3rd Motorized Rifle Battalion, Dániel Csorba fought with the 15th Bicycle Battalion, reserve military doctor Csaba Vargha accompanied with the III Short Range Reconnaissance Squadron.

I also attached photos from the Hungarian War Correspondent Company, an official propaganda unit organized in 1940-1941 to document the war from an official point of view, boosting the morale of the Army and the Hungarian population.

The photographs on the one hand documented the individual and small unit history of the advancing Hungarian troops, showing their equipment, weaponry as well as picturing the difficulties, casualties, and fatigue of the war. On the other hand, the Hungarians had taken photos of the enemy too. These selected photos display the hostile terrain, the demolished bridges, abandoned and destroyed Soviet vehicles, planes, and weapons as well as the prisoners of war, local civilians. The Hungarians were shocked by the everyday life of the Soviet system, the poverty of the local population, and the grandiose industrial sites surrounded by shanty towns of the workers. Unintentionally the photographers also showed the brutality of the war, which inflicted unbearable pain on the civilian population, which trapped among the Axis forces, Red Army, and the partisans.

Operation Barbarossa and Hungary

Operation Barbarossa

Early hours of 22 June 1941, under the codename of "Barbarossa" Germany and its allies attacked the Soviet Union. This conflict, which fought on the Eastern Front, was a total war, fought by all elements of the involving societies, because both sides aimed "to exterminate the opponent, to destroy his political existence". Performing this total war meant cruelty, throwing away the century's old rules of war. This conflict imposed unnecessary suffering on civilians as well as soldiers and prisoners of war.

Although, since August 1939 a German/Soviet non–aggression pact existed, it was clear for both sides that the war would be inevitable with each other. The Soviets hoped that the western powers and Nazi Germany would wear down each other and in the end, they could conquer Europe at minimum cost. But the Soviet Armed Forces was not yet ready for the war in 1941; Stalin had to keep playing for time.

Hitler's intention to invade the Soviet Union was based on ideological and economic reasons. The Germans also recognized that sooner or later the war with the Red giant would be unavoidable. The numbers of the opposing forces clearly stated the numerical superiority of the Soviet Army of the Western Military districts itself.

At the time of the attack, approximately 3.6 million German and Axis soldiers with 3600 armored vehicles,

This photograph epitomizes the main goal of Hungary during WW2, regain and preserve the territories lost due to WW1. Admiral Miklós Horthy, governor of the Kingdom of Hungary arrived at Marosvásárhely (Satu Mare) during the reconquest of Northern-Transylvania on 16 September 1940. [Fortepan /9345]

The Peace Treaty of Trianon and the catastrophic financial state of Hungary severely restricted the military capability of the Hungarian Army. The Army was armed equipped and clothed according to the WW1 standards in the early 30s. Hungarian infantry unit parades at Veszprém still wearing the old 17M steel helmets. [P. Mujzer]

7100 artillery pieces, and 2700 aircraft crossed the Soviet frontier. At the beginning of the operations, the Red Army had 2.9 million soldiers, 15000 armored vehicles, 35000 artillery pieces, and 8500 planes to counter the invaders. This formidable war machine soon melted away under the Axis onslaught. Until the end of the year, almost 20000 Soviet armored vehicles, the majority of the aircraft's were mostly destroyed on the ground, some 4 million Red Army men perished; 80% of the total strength of the Soviet Armed forces.

Officers and men of a machine gun company in the early 30s, the soldiers still dressed in the old style uniform with standing collar. The company commander and the senior NCO wear their WW1 decorations. Their weapon is the aging 8mm 07/31M Schwarzlose machine gun also inherited from WW1. [Fortepan/Bakó]

The Hungarian field artillery was mostly equipped with horse-drawn WW1 artillery pieces. The 15cm 14M medium field howitzer was transported in two separate sections. The barrel section of the howitzer attached to the limber is towed by six horses. [Fortepan/Konok id]

The Axis forces were divided into three Army Groups; each Group had its territorial objectives, however, the main aim was to trap and annihilate the Red Army, preferably within 400-500 kilometers of the border, in the European part of the Soviet Union. The planning staff wanted to avoid that the Soviets might

Hungarian soldiers of the experimental Motorised Group posing on a Rába truck in the early 30s, dressed in light-weighted summer uniform, armed with 31M Manlicher carbines, it was the re-chambered version of the 95M Manlicher rifle. [Markó]

From the mid-30s the Army started to purchase modern equipment and armament from abroad. Hungarian signal men fix the radio mast of a Henschel 33 D1 (Kfz 72) signal truck used by signal battalions that belonged to corps and army level. [Fortepan/Konok id]

fall back deep into the interior of the country to perform a battle of attrition on the edge of Asia, in Siberia.

From our topic of interest is the Army Group South, and then commanded by Field Marshal Gerd von Rundstedt. His Army Group aim was to destroy the Soviet forces in Galicia and Western Ukraine by a swift strike from the area of Lublin to Kiev, crossing the River Dnieper, and then advancing rapidly southeast along the

On battalion and company level the troops used Hungarian-made field radio and telephone sets. Signalmen practice with an R/3 radio set, the radio had an arch antenna and was supplied by a hand-operated generator. [Fortepan/Erky-Nagy]

River, in a single envelopment, preventing the escape of the units of the Red Army.

The Army Group South consisted of three armies along the Soviet-Polish border north and west of Lvov. The Armoured Group 1, led by General Ewald von Kleist, supported by the 6th Army, commanded by Field Marshal Walter von Reichenau would strike east of Kiev. The 17th Army, under General Carl Heinrich von Stülpnagel, attacked southeast past Lvov toward Vinnitsa. The 11th Army, commanded by General Eugen Ritter von Schobert attacked out of Romanian territory to the northeast accompanied by Romanian forces. It aimed to meet the units of the 17th Army around the area of Vinnitsa.

Between the 17th and 11th German Armies laid a gap running along the mountainous terrain of the Carpathian Mountain that belonged to the then neutral Hungarian Kingdom.

The Army Group South manpower had the highest number added non-German Forces; 325000 Romanian troops, later on, augmented with 96000 Hungarian, 62000 Italian, and 45000 Slovakian soldiers.

The opposing Soviet forces were better prepared than the other Red Army units along the border. On the one hand, the Soviet planners expected in case of a German attack, the main weight of the enemy offensive south of the Pripet Marshes. So the Soviets allocated strong forces in this area. On the other hand, the local Soviet commander risked Stalin's displeasure by ordering some defensive preparation, following the deteriorating situation in the weeks before the war started.

The Kiev Military District, under the leadership of Colonel-General Kirponos, was responsible for manning the 940km long line of defense. The Soviet troops were deployed in four armies, from north to south the 5th, 6th, 26th, and 12th Armies. The 12th Soviet Army was

The Hungarians purchased the 105mm German leFH 18 light field howitzers, put into service as 37M light howitzer. The mechanized version used by artillery battalions of the Mobile Corps, the horses drawn ones belonged to the infantry brigades' artillery. [Fortepan/Djemil]

The Army purchased Italian CV 35 tankettes in the mid-30s, called 35M Fiat Ansaldo, and armed with twin 8mm 34AM Gebauer machine guns. Ansaldo tank demonstrates its obstacle-crossing ability. By the early 40s, the tankettes were outdated for combat operation. [Fortepan/Zagyva]

35M Fiat Ansaldo tankettes of the Tankette Company of the 1st Cavalry Brigade and a Hussar Squadron wait for the marching order during the operation against Slovakia in March 1939. That time the white triangle unit sign belonged to the 1st Cavalry Brigade's Tankette Company, which later was developed into an armored cavalry battalion. [P. Mujzer]

located on the Soviet-Hungarian border, from Borislav to Kamenyec-Podolszk. The Soviet Southwest Front had 907.000 men in arms. The armored fist of the Soviet forces consisted of eight mechanized corps.

The German attacks meet stiff resistance on the River Bug and in front of Lvov(Lemberg). The southern flank of the Armoured Group 1 was subject to series of Soviet counter-attacks, which temporarily halted its advance.

As far as the terrain was concerned, there were significant River obstacles, especially the River Bug on the Polish border, the river Dniester facing Romania, and the River Dnieper. The impassable Pripet Marshes also

The Hungarian military industry also started to produce homemade armored vehicles, the 39M Csaba armored car was designed by the Weiss Manfred Factory and the Military Technology Institute based on the plans of engineer Nicholas Strausler, who emigrated to the UK before the war. [Fortepan/Csorba]

39M Csaba armored car belonged to the 1st Reconnaissance Battalion with white Maltese cross military insignia during the occupation of Transylvania in September 1940. In front of the armored car is a Hungarian 37mm 36M (Pak 36) anti-tank gun. [Fortepan/Erky-Nagy]

One of the best designs of the Hungarian war industry was the 38M Botond all-terrain squad carrier truck, capable to transport 12 riflemen and the driver and co-driver. The first series of Botond trucks were right-hand drives and handed over to the troops in the summer of 1940. [Fortepan/ Erky-Nagy]

Rail transportation of the Heavy Weapon Company of the 15th Bicycle Battalion, returning to their garrison after the occupation of Transylvania. The company commander playing card with his subordinates on a flat car packed with Krupp Protze truck and Schwarzlose machine gun. [Fortepan/Csorba]

The Hungarians produced under license the Swedish Bofors anti-aircraft gun as 40mm 36M Bofors autocannon one of the best artillery weapons of the Army. The Mobile Troops had one battery of six Boffors autocannons per brigades towed by 37M Hans Lloyd half-tracked tractors. [Fortepan]

constituted a sort of hazard on the northern flank of the Army Group South, where it joined to the right flank of Army Group Centre. The land was largely flat, except the starting operational area of the Hungarian forces, which laid in the Carpathian Mountains. The road networks in the Carpathian Mountains were limited to only a few passable roads and railways going through valleys and passes. Otherwise, the terrain was ideal for conducting mobile warfare in case of dry weather, a mix of trees and bushes in the northern areas giving way to treeless plains and agricultural fields in the south. However, in the case of rainy weather in spring and autumn, the soil produced

The 80mm 29M Bofors anti-aircraft gun was the backbone of the anti-aircraft artillery, also manufactured under Swedish license. Due to the peace treaty restriction, this anti-aircraft gun was manned by the crew that belonged to the River Forces in the early 30s at the firing range of Várpalota. [P. Mujzer]

The 29M Bofors anti-aircraft guns towed by the Hungarian produced KV-40 artillery tractors. The tractor towed the gun and the limber. The 29M Bofors gun was accurate, but a static weapon, to make it ready for the fire was time-consuming. [Fortepan/Kakuk]

particularly nasty mud, which evaporated slowly. As the temperature rose and fell the so-called roads alternately turned into impassable quagmires or frozen solid rocks. Although the road network existed since the Habsburg Empire on the former Polish territories, in a big picture, by European standards roads not existed; the highways were few and at best had a sort of stone surface with huge potholes. The railway gauges were different from the European standard, much wider, so the supply must reload on the border of the Soviet Union, which complicated the supply chain during the whole war.

Hungary in 1941

At the end of the First World War, Hungary, as a member of the k. und k. Monarchy ended up on the losing side. Her army disintegrated and her armaments were either taken over or destroyed by the victorious Allied nations. In the autumn of 1919, after the failure of a short-lived Soviet-style republic, a new Hungarian National Army was organized under French supervision. This army was led by a former k. und k. admiral, the highest-ranking native Hungarian military officer, Admiral Miklós Horthy, who was later (in 1920) to become Regent of Hungary, ruling in place of the deposed Habsburgs. Hungary never officially renounced its status as a monarchy, and effectively the nation remained a monarchy without a king until the end of the Second World War.

After WWI, Hungary was in a very critical situation. In 1920 the Allied Powers gave the Hungarian delegation their conditions for peace. This agreement, the Treaty of Trianon, was very similar to the one already imposed on Germany at Versailles, and a French General was later to state that the only result

37M Hansa Lloyd's half-tracked artillery tractor belonged to the artillery units of the Mobile Corps towing the 36M Bofors autocannons and the 37M light howitzers. The white chevron with dot was the unit sign of the 1st Motorised Artillery Battalion, which belonged to the 1st Motorised Rifle Brigade. [Fortepan/Mikó]

A broken down Hansa Lloyd artillery tractor recovered by a 38M Toldi light tank belonged to the 1st Armoured Cavalry Battalion during the Yugoslavian Campaign in April 1941. The white Turul bird with a sword was the unit sign of the Light Tank Company of the 1st Armoured Cavalry Battalion. [Fortepan/Hajdú Fedő]

The 38M Toldi light tank was the license production of the L-60 Swedish tank. The 38M Toldi light tank was very mobile but with thin armor and light 20mm armament, capable of reconnaissance only. Officer candidates trained in the position of the gunner and commander in the turret of the Toldi tank. [Fortepan/Ludovika]

The new armored vehicles, the 38M Toldi light tanks, and the 39M Csaba armored cars were put into service in the summer of 1940, taking part in the occupation of Transylvania. These armored vehicles belonged to the 1st Reconnaissance Battalion, wearing the unit white Maltese cross military insignia and the white lightning bolt unit insignia, in front of the vehicles standing an Air Force captain. [Fortepan/Varga dr.]

Hussar radio team prepared for exercise, the R/2 radio set, and the generator carry on a packhorse. The cavalry radio team could keep up with a hussar squadron in any circumstances providing communication among the troops and commanders. [P. Mujzer]

By early 1941 the Hungarian Mobile Troops consisted of cavalry, bicycle, motorized rifle, reconnaissance, and armored battalions organized into the Mobile Corps. Parading troops of the 10th Bicycle Battalion and motorized rifles riding on 38M Botond trucks marching at Budapest in April 1941. The cyclist on the left carrying the R/1 platoon radio set on his back. [Fortepan/Divéky]

was a twenty-year-long cease-fire, nothing more. The peace conditions for Hungary reduced the area of the country from 282,000 square kilometers to 93,000 square kilometers and the population from 18 million to 9.5 million. Thus 3,263,000 Hungarians became citizens of foreign countries under hostile administrations. The provisions of the Treaty of Trianon reduced Hungary's 1914 industrial base by about 80%.

The Treaty of Trianon was a huge shock for the whole society. The Treaty has left a never-ending scar on the Hungarian national consciousness. Everybody was affected, at least emotionally by the harsh conditions of the Treaty. Hungary had lost its imperial status and was reduced to a small country surrounded by hostile states.

It was evident from the very beginning that the nation would not follow these dictates if they could be

Staff car carrying the battle flag of the 10th Bicycle Battalion attached to the trumpet, the unit sign a white triangle painted on the right mudguard. The dispatch riders wear their leather protective gear and Italian-style crash helmet. Two of them riding the Puch G350 motorbike, the third one is a requisitioned civilian motorcycle. [Fortepan/Divéky]

Hungarian bicycle troops lined up with their fully kitted 32M military bicycles produced by the Weiss Manfred Factory. The equipment of the soldiers; blanket roll, backpack, entrenching tool, half poncho secured to their bicycles. They are also carrying an extra metal ammunition box for their 31M squad light machine gun. Each ammunition box contains five spare magazines or bulk cartridges. [Fortepan/Divéky]

circumvented. Hungarian foreign policy made no secret that it aimed to regain the lost territories. Hungary signed the Treaty of Trianon on 4th June 1920 because it had no other alternative, but her goal was to invalidate the Treaty as soon as possible.

Hungarian diplomacy worked to form a close Italian, Austrian and Hungarian relationship in the late 1920s and early 1930s, to avoid isolation and to try to create a better position for Hungary among the European nations. In 1927 Hungary signed a treaty of co-operation with Italy. In the mid-1930s the international political situation changed. Germany had invalidated the Treaty of Versailles and begun to build up a modern regular army. To the Hungarians, Germany seemed to present the opportunity for a good alliance, perhaps providing the only support

Hungarian Krupp Protze half squad carrier truck of the Heavy Weapon Company belongs to the 10th Bicycle Battalion, passing the motorized rifles riding on their 38M Botond trucks in April 1941. Interestingly the driver of the Krupp Protze wears an Italian-style crash helmet. The heavy weapon companies of the bicycle battalions had six machine guns and two mortars. [Fortepan/Divéky]

Mercedes G5 medium command car of the 10th Bicycle Battalion, the unit sig also painted on the right mudguard, next to the driver a 2nd lieutenant is sitting in the car. On the back seat are the radio operator and his R/2 radio set. [Fortepan/Divéky]

Fiat 508 Coloniale small command car belongs to the 1st Reconnaissance Battalion, white lightning bolt unit insignia painted on the right mudguard of the car. Carrying stick bundles to help out the car from possible potholes. [Fortepan/Divéky]

that Hungary could expect in its quest to recoup her losses of WWI.

As previously stated, Hungary's main aim was to regain her lost territories, especially those where Hungarians lived as a majority. However, the military leadership had no illusions about the real potential of the Hungarian Armed Forces. That is why Hungary first focused on a political solution and looked at a military solution as secondary. A comparison of the strengths of the Little Entente's forces with the Hungarian Army reveals the significant differences in size and armaments.

In November of 1938, after the Munich Agreement the Hungarians, due to the Vienna Arbitrage regained Upper-Hungary from Czechoslovakia.

The Hungarians occupied Carpathian-Ukraine by force against the Slovakians in March 1939. The next step was the conflict with Romania for Transylvania. The tension between Hungary and Romania reached a peak in the summer of 1940, owing to Romania's failure to

Bicycle troopers of the 10th Bicycle Battalion passing the 38M Botond trucks of the 3rd Motorised Rifle Battalion. The unit sign, the vertical white stripe painted on the right mudguard of the Botond truck. The cyclist third from right carrying his 31M light machine gun attached to the frame of the bicycle, the stock of the weapon is visible under the blanket roll. [Fortepan/Divéky]

respond to Hungarian claims to the disputed area of Transylvania. The possibility of a conflict was against the German interest, they intervened and the second Vienna Arbitrage decided that one part of Transylvania was given back to Hungary. The last step on the road to regaining the lost territory was the participation in the Balkan Campaign against Yugoslavia. In this case, Hungarians gained again former Hungarian territories by force and casualties.

In exchange for the German political and military support, Hungary had to pay dearly to the Third Reich. In November 1940 Hungary signed an alliance agreement with the Germans which gave them extra rights them. According to the Axis Alliance Pact, the Germans demanded close political, economical and military cooperation between Hungary and the Third Reich. This practically meant benefits for the Germans in return for their support during the recovery of the lost Hungarian territories. The German troops could freely transit through and station in Hungary. The Germans had the monopoly to acquire Hungarian industrial and agricultural products. The Hungarian government also follow Germany's racial agenda against their own Jews citizens. This led to the mass deportation of the Hungarian Jews community in the summer of 1944.

However, the Germans did not plan to involve directly the Hungarians in the Barbarossa Campaign. Original the Hungarian role was to be a secure communication line, logistic, supply base behind the operational area.

Hungarian Army

The Hungarian Armed Forces between the Wars

The Hungarian Army, due to the limitations imposed by the Trianon Treaty, was unable to protect the country. The available manpower was just enough to maintain internal security following the requirements of the Little Entente states Czechoslovakia, Yugoslavia, and Romania. The basic formation of the Army became the mixed brigade, of which seven were organized. The Army also formed four cavalry/hussar regiments and a few support units to arrive at the permitted total of 35.000 men.

The plan was to establish a flexible, powerful, and not too expensive basic formation, which later could be used as the cadre for expansion to a larger army. The mixed brigades were composed of two infantry regiments, one artillery, and one cyclist battalion, mortar and cavalry companies plus support units. Seven brigades were organized and were allocated to seven military districts within Hungary. These districts were headquartered at Budapest (1st), Székesfehérvár (2nd), Szombathely (3rd), Pécs (4th), Szeged (5th), Debrecen (6th), and at Miskolc (7th). However, the Hungarian government and military leadership recognized that these units could not protect Hungary. Following Germany's example, the Hungarian Army began to organize secret units, and to conceal war materials, in direct violation of the dictates of the Trianon Treaty. These extra units were hidden in the branches of the State Police, Customs Service, Gendarmerie, and other non-combatant governmental and non-governmental entities such as shipping companies and airlines.

Medical check-up of the Hungarian soldiers behind a Ford BB (Kfz.31) ambulance truck. At the mobile troops, the battalion aid stations had one or two ambulance trucks and a supply truck carrying the medical staff and equipment. The Ford BB was produced with Hungarian chassis made by Uhry Factory. [Fortepan/Ludovika]

The Hungarian Army had a huge number of well-trained officers, both professionals, and reservists, who had gained valuable experience in the k. und k. Army in WWI. Many wished to serve, but in an army that was only one-tenth the size of the k. und k. Army, only a small percent of them could serve in true military units, while the rest were passed to non-military, governmental duties.

The armaments originated from the k. und k. Army, and as such were much worn due to their extensive use during WWI. Forbidden heavy artillery pieces, armored trains, and other prohibited weapons were concealed all around Hungary in civilian stores, cellars, or simply dug under the earth to conceal them from the Allied Military Committee. The Hungarian State Railways (MÁV) played a major role in this hid and seek game. Train loads of forbidden materials were transported all around Hungary.

102nd Armoured Train during the occupation of Transylvania, the Hungarians inherited armored trains from the Monarchy, hiding them and later rearmed and modernized to some extent. The armored trains also belonged to the Mobile Troops. The artillery wagon was armed with an 80mm light gun in the main turret, one 20mm anti-tank rifle in a small turret, and machine guns. [Fortepan/Kokány]

Hungarian-Soviet Border Post at Uzhok, the Carpathian Mountains, Hungarian mountain jagers wearing their distinctive visor hat field cap. Behind them is an ex-Polish wz.34 half-tracked tractors used by the Hungarians in the Carpathian region in 1940. [Fortepan/Urbán]

Hungarian Frontier Guard troopers training with an ex-Czechoslovak 37mm anti-tank gun captured from the Yugoslavian Army in April 1941. The soldiers belonged to the mountain-equipped frontier guard battalion protecting the mountainous region of Carpathian-Ruthenia. [P. Mujzer]

The Hungarian corps artillery had one horse draw and on motorized medium howitzer battalion. The 150cm 31M howitzer and its limber were towed by a 26M Pavesi artillery tractor. This howitzer was manufactured under the license of the Swedish Bofors Factory in Hungary. [Fortepan/Konok id.]

Unfortunately, the result of these improper storage conditions was that the majority of the weapons, ammunitions were damaged, rusted and unsuitable for use in case of war.

The output of Hungarian military industries was either confiscated by Romanian forces in 1920 or destroyed by the Allied Military Committee. The greatest problem of the Hungarian Army was its very poor financial condition, which created a serious obstacle to modernization and enlargement. Starting in 1927, the pressure from the Allied Committee lessened, and the constant supervision ended.

The Enlargement of the Hungarian Army

During the secret rearmament, the Hungarian Army initially concentrated on enlarging the personnel strength and building up a supply of the equipment forbidden by the Treaty of Trianon. Starting in the mid-thirties, Hungary had a chance to purchase weapons and armaments from Italy and Germany and neutral countries such as Sweden and Switzerland. The home-based military industry was also enlarged following the overall economic situation. By 1938 the Hungarian Army had seven mixed brigades, one cavalry division, (two hussar brigades,) an aviation brigade, an experimental motorized group, and the River Forces. Under the direct command of the Chief of the General Staff were two heavy artillery battalions, four anti-aircraft artillery battalions, one signal battalion, one chemical warfare battalion, a mechanized transport regiment, and an armored group.

The total strength was 85,000 men, two and a half times more than permitted by the peace treaty. 1938 brought a decisive change in the Hungarian Army's situation and development. Relying on the German-Italian alliance, and backed by the Polish and Austrian governments, the Hungarian Government revealed its rearmament program.

On March of 5, 1938, Prime Minister Kálmán Darányi announced his government's 1 billion Pengő rearmament program which, disregarding political and financial barriers, was aimed at accelerating the rebuilding of the national defense system within 3-5 years. This rearmament program dealt mainly with the enlargement of the mobile troops and the air force. In the 1936-1937 budget years, the national budget of Hungary was 4.417 million Pengő (almost $1.3 million with an exchange rate at that time of 1 USD equalling 3.40 Pengő).

This plan provided a boost not only to the army but also to the country as a whole, generating many new investments and jobs, not just in the military industry. Recognition by the Little Entente states that, from their point of view, the international situation had deteriorated led them to negotiate an equal rearmament pact with Hungary, which was signed in a small Yugoslavian town, Bled on 22 August 1938. As of this time, Hungary's rearmament was legal. However, there remained the problem of the impoverished state of the nation.

After the signature of the Bled equal rearmament treaty, Hungary speeded up the enlarging of its army.

Hungarian reserve officer candidates of a Hussar unit take riding lessons, wearing light-weighted summer uniforms. The cavalry consisted of four hussar regiments and independent hussar squadrons belonged to the infantry brigades and corps. [Fortepan/Zagyva]

Hungarian rifle company lead by an ensign, platoon commander in 1941. The soldiers were armed with 35M rifles, and 31M light machine guns, per regulations a rifle company had 12 light machine guns distributed among four rifle platoons. [Fortepan/Kokány]

The former mixed brigades were expanded to form infantry corps, each with three infantry brigades. The final enlargement plan, called the "Huba Plan", called for the establishment of the following units by 1942:

25 infantry brigades, each consisting of two infantry regiments

1 cavalry and two armored divisions

2 mountain brigades

1 frontier guard brigade

1 River forces brigade

2 air force brigades

Conscription system

Due to the restriction of the post-WW1 Peace Treaty of Trianon, the Hungarian Army must base on the contracted soldiers. It lasted until the mid-30s when more and more young men were involved in the military service. From 1938, according to the equal rearmament pact, officially the Hungarian Armed Forces switched on the compulsory military service for the male population between 18 and 60.

Pre-conscription training

The Hungarian compulsory pre-military "*Levente*" training was similar to the European systems, where the States prepared their citizens for their duty to serve in the Army. The "Levente" organization officially targeted the physical fitness and the patriot indoctrination of the Hungarian males from the age of 12 until the conscription. It was organized and executed by reserve officers, very likely the village teachers and NCOs. The training program focused on basic infantry training, drill exercises, marching in formation, marksmanship with small-caliber so-called "Levente" rifles. The training was given on Sundays, not always appreciated by the candidates; however, the absence was an offense.

Conscription

At age of 21, later at 19, men undertook three years-long military service before transferred to the 1st (under age 42), 2nd (between the age of 42 and 48), and 3rd Reserve (until the age of 65).

Hungary was predominantly an agricultural country between the Wars; enlisted men mostly came from the countryside. They were accustomed to the hardship of heavy labor under the open air, could handle horses, carts which were the main way of transportation in the Army. The skilled workers of the industry were so precious that a significant part of them was not mobilized because their expertise was needed in the military industry. A significant Jewish population lived in Hungary; they averagely were more educated occupying middle-class positions in the society. Until 1940 they conscripted into the Armed Forces as any Hungarian citizens. Even so, due to their skill and education, they were more likely to be able to drive, handle communication equipment and other, more complicated systems. But the Hungarian government in harmony with the Nazi Reich already proclaimed the so-called "Jewish Acts" in 1938-1944. These legal and administrative rules made the Hungarian Jews' life hard and difficult. Their businesses were taken over by the Hungarian State. The Jews were downgraded to second-class citizens. From 1940 they were not allowed to serve in combat troops, they were drafted into labor companies.

Due to the regained territories of the former Hungarian Kingdom, the population of Hungary changed significantly. The whole population was 14,6 million people, about 81% were Hungarians, half-half million German and Ruthenia (Carpathian-Ukrainian), one million Romanian and a quarter million former Yugoslavian people lived in Hungary as minorities. The male component of this almost three million people was eligible for military service. Except for the German minorities, their incorporation into the Army generated problems. First of all the language barriers were difficult to overcome. Contrary to the old K. und K. system, the Hungarian commanding officers and NCOs did not speak the language of their men. The conscripts were forced to learn in Hungarian, but they were not willing to do so. The so-called protected units like Air Force, mechanized troops were exempted to draft minorities into their unit. On the other hand, it increased the number of non native soldiers belongs to the line infantry. Even these units used the soldiers with minority backgrounds for non-combatant roles, supply service, labor units. This kind of approach is based on mutual distrust. However, in the case of a dedicated commander, the minorities were as good and loyal as the native Hungarians. The Slovakian and Ruthenian conscripts or Hungarian comrades, who spoken these languages could use their skills to communicate with the local population or interrogate prisoners and carry out clandestine reconnaissance patrols in Ukraine.

Based on the pre-military training records, in early summer, when the young men attained the conscription age was called to conscription boards chaired by officers and a doctor. The candidates were interviewed and assigned to a selected branch according to the needs of the branches and the qualification of the conscripts. The call-in order just arrived in October, after the end of the summer agricultural activities. By that time the man power was a critical factor of the harvesting.

Enlisted training

The training period lasted from October to next year October. Theoretically, the freshly drafted conscripts were already had their drill during the compulsory pre-military training. The freshly drafted conscripts started their two months of basic training at their respective units, no special training unit was dedicated to this role. Within the regiments/battalions, training companies formed under the supervision of NCOs and

Land tail of an aviation squadron equipped with requisitioned civilian Hanomag Sturm car and Italian Isotta-Fraschini D70 heavy military trucks with trailers. The enlisted men wear the beret and the older reserve officers had their regular Air Force officer uniform with visor hats. [Fortepan/Fadgyas]

junior officers, to teach them the drill and basic infantry skills. The basic training included; drill movement in section, platoon, and company level, individual weapon handling of the 31M and 35M rifles, marching exercise, and small unit tactics.

At the end of the basic training, the conscripts taken the oath during a military pared at the garrison. Then the specialized training started for the enlisted men. The promising candidates were selected for section leader training, which took an extra 4-6 months at the battalion level.

The Mountain Jager and mountain-equipped Border Guard units had their normal infantry training augmented by special training methods and courses reflected on the requirements of the mountain warfare. The first Mountain Training Course was organized in 1939 following the regained mountainous territory of Hungary to provide skilled forces for the border defense of this region. These units were kitted, uniformed, and equipped with special items suited for mountain warfare.

The specialized training at the Mobile Corps connected to the means of transportation of the troops. As Hungary was predominantly an agricultural country, handling and riding horses was not too difficult for the village boys. On the other hand, to learn cycling was much demanding, just a few boys could learn to cycle at home. Operating motor vehicles, trucks, even so, armored vehicles needed more educated enlisted men with skills and training. The military leadership was aware of the vulnerability and the relatively high costs of the Mobile Forces in case of war, tried to save them.

The Hussars had their old, traditional cavalry training upgraded with the use of new weapons and equipment. However, the cavalry was the most vulnerable part of the Mobile Corps due to a lot of horses which made supply and deployments difficult.

The motorized rifle battalions were converted from the field jager battalions and grenadier companies, a kind of elite light infantry force. Their tactical training was based on a more independent, flexible mission-oriented training, which was utilized during the conversion. They were familiarised with the new method of transportation, mainly the Hungarian made 38M Botond all-terrain squad carrier truck, practicing the movement and deployments from trucks in combat.

At the bicycle battalions next to the traditional infantry training, focused on long-range cycling exercises with a full kit for the bicyclist troops. The bicycle battalions were the most complex units of the Mobile Troops, containing bicycle, motorized, tankett, and light howitzer elements too. It was important practicing and coordinate the movements and deployments of the different elements in changeable tactical situations.

NCO training

The professional NCOs were trained at the Kinizsi Pál NCN School at Veszprém/Juttas from 1924 until 1944. The NCO School had one-one infantry, artillery, and mobile training battalion. The mobile battalion consisted of one-one cavalry and armored companies. From 1934, selected enlisted men could apply to the NCO School. The two years-long training course was famously thought and demanding. The graduates were respected and feared by the conscripts and valued by the officers.

The junior NCOs were selected and trained at the troops on battalion/regiment level NCO courses. However, the Army was always short of well-trained NCOs which harmed the operations.

Reserve officer training

According to the Hungarian system, conscripted personals with grammar school degrees were entitled to serve and train as reserve officers. During the first year, they were trained to be reserve officer candidates at their units. Every regiment had its own "one year volunteers' school". The officer candidates were trained to be troop or platoon commanders at their regiment. At the end of this one-year course, they were promoted to the rank of officer candidate sergeant. During the next conscripted year they served as a platoon commander. Later on, they were several times recall, for short periods to the Army and were promoted to reserve ensigns or 2nd Lieutenants The constant lack of manpower at the Officer Corps allowed reserve officers and officer candidates to apply to the Professional Officer Corps.

At least two classes of conscripts were in active service, sometimes, depending upon the degree of mobilization more. The men who had been trained in one formation were always called up to that same formation either with the rest of their class or individually, for active duty when they needed.

Commissioned Officers

To serve in the Army as a commissioned officer was regarded very prestigious and financially stable job. Independent military education in Hungary dated back to the 19th Century. The Ludovika Military Academy was established for the training of native Hungarian officer candidates within the k. und k. Monarchy. After

WWI the Ludovika trained officers for the Hungarian Armed Forces. The curriculum at the Ludovika consisted of one-year enlisted training at their respective branch of the candidates and three years long academic studies.

As regards mobile forces, cavalry and horse artillery officer training courses were already being taught from the beginning. In the 1930s, with the recognition of the importance of mobile warfare, bicycle, motorized, and armored officer training was established. From 1939, a Mobile Warfare Group was organized for cavalry, bicycle, and armored officer candidates. The Mobile Warfare Group consisted of one-one cavalry, bicycle, and armored companies. In 1940, a separate class was organized for the armored cadets.

The specialized training of the motorized rifle officers started in 1941. The motorized rifles are differentiated from the normal infantry that they moved by vehicles but fight on foot like the infantry troops. In the beginning, the grenadier and jäger officers and men were retrained as motorized rifles. When the bicycle battalions were converted into tank battalions their officers were also retrained as armored ones.

The officers of the mountain and mountain-equipped border guard units were retrained infantry officers, later mountain officer courses were organized within the infantry officer training at the Ludovika Military Academy.

The Army Staff, the brain of the army was also forbidden by the Treaty of Trianon but existed from the beginning under cover institutes. Later it was named War College where the most talented and dedicated young Captains were trained to be staff officers.

The senior officers of the Hungarian Army were trained and served in the K. und K. Armee before and during WW1. However, due to the limitations of the Peace Treaty, a lot of them were in cover positions for years not working with troops. When the enlargement of the Army started they returned to the active service.

The Hungarian Army inherited, not just the traditions, most of the weapons, equipment, but the military thinking of the K. und K. Armee, which was not a surprise taking into consideration that the military leadership trained, served, and fought in the K. und K. Army during WW1. The training and tactical manuals were harmonized and upgraded per the new challenges of the 30s. However, the training and the internal life of the Hungarian Army were not significantly changed since WW1.

The training was overshadowed on every level by the lack of ammunition, fuel, training weapons, exercises, and maneuvers. The new weapons and vehicles were also saved from training to avoid wearing them down. On the other hand, the lack of training back lashed in case of operation. Due to the financial restriction, no large-scale maneuvers were held before 1938. However, the peaceful recovery of the lost territory offered large-scale military movements for the military leadership as well as for the troop level officers and men too.

Logistic

The state of the living conditions (barracks, garrisons), the quality and quantity of the food, clothing, and sanitation by East-European standards were normal, acceptable in the Hungarian Army. These standards are based on the old K. und K. Armee standards.

In case of mobilization, the reservist headed towards their garrisons, their movements were hampered by heavy traffic. The affected units franticly worked to achieve the readiness in time. A significant part of the supply columns had civilian horses, carts, and motor vehicles, which were called in case of mobilization. The movement control units and the Railway Traffic Coordination Centre worked to plan harmonize and execute the railway and road traffic to deliver the troops by train as close as possible to the assembly areas. The narrow supply road in the Carpathian Mountains caused a never-ending traffic jam, the supply column separated from the troops which could not get their rations in time. Based on a German-Hungarian agreement the Germans supplied the Hungarians with food, fuel, and ammunition, spare parts of German origin in Hungarian service. However, the majority of the Hungarian re-supply should have arrived from Hungary. In urgent cases ammunition, food was air delivered to the fighting troops.

The Hungarian military cousin is based on traditional Hungarian meals. The hot meals were cooked at battalion/company level kitchens and served for the troops. In case of exercise or operation, hot meals were prepared in a two-wheeled field kitchen called goulash canon. Normally beef and pork stew was cooked for the troops. Theoretically, one day of field food ration per man consisted of 700-gram bread, 300-gram meat, 200 gram preserved vegetables, and grease.

The emergency field rations of the soldiers consisted of sea biscuits and canned meats kept in their field pack. It could be eaten on order by the commanding officer.

According to the regulation on battalion level 6 days of food supply had to keep at the battalion supply column. However, normally just one day supply was at

Fiat Cr.32 fighter biplane belonged to the 1/2 Fighter Squadron with reserve 2nd Lieutenant Antal Bánhidi, a famous Hungarian aviator sitting in the cockpit. The plane had the V.122 tactical number and the "Lúdas Matyi" unit emblem. [Fortepan/Erky-Nagy]

the battalions. The troops had to live on the field, what they found, confiscated, or captured from the enemy and the local population. Ukraine was the so-called "bread basket" of the Soviet Union with huge agricultural lands and farms and endless villages. In the summertime, there were a lot of fruits, vegetables, poultry, and pigs to improve the field rations. According to the enlisted men's memories after the mere survival, the quantity and quality of the food was the second most important issue. The looting of the civilians was a serious, punishable military crime in the Hungarian Army too, but the supply shortfall should be addressed. The quartermasters tried to formalize the on-the-spot supply by focusing on the captured and abandoned Soviet military and State-owned sources. Very soon a kind of black market developed between the troopers and the locals, where the peoples exchanged eggs, fruits, poultry for cigarettes, canned rations.

Medical care was according to the East-European standard. At the company level, one medical orderly and stretcher-bearers were trained. The dressing instruments and procedures were outdated. On battalion level medical first aid post normaly organized with one-two junior, reserve medical officer in charge, and medical orderlies. According to the regulations, medical evacuation columns and field hospitals were organized on a higher level. The wounded soldiers were treated on company or battalion level according to the seriousness of their injuries and transported back to the first aid / medical station where the life-saving treatments were done, fixing the broken legs, arms, amputations, proper dressing, etc. Then the wounded were transported by medical evacuation column to the field hospitals where the hospital-level medical care was executed.

However, during the first 5 days of the operation, the VIII Corps had no medical institute, due to the slow mobilization, the 24th Medical Column just arrived on 30 June and 1-2 days needed to be operationally ready. It had fatal consequences in case of medium or serious injuries.

Armament of the Hungarian Army in 1941

Most of the Hungarian infantry weapons were inherited from the old K. und K. arsenal or based on developed from these weapons.

Small arms

Besides the officers and NCOs, due to the lack of rifles, the support and supply personals were also armed with service pistols for self-protection. In the late 20s, the Army decided to replace the mixed WW1 and Frommer Stop pistols with a simpler and unified hand weapon. The Frommer offered his 9mm pistol, a simple and robust blow-back weapon, serviceable and reliable, and went into service as a 29M service pistol produced by FÉG Factory. Due to the expansive interest of the Army, a modified pistol the 37M was developed and accepted by the Army. It was an upgrade of the previous one produced in large quantity for German export too. The pistol weighed 765g, had a 7-round detachable box magazine, with a muzzle velocity of 290m/second.

In 1941 the Hungarian Army was equipped with the 95M, 31M, and 35M service rifles. The Hungarian Army retained the 95M straight-pull 8mm Manlicher rifle until adopted a new cartridge in 1931, named Manlicher 31M rifle. The original 95M rifles were re-barrelled in great quantities to take the new cartridge. However, the new cartridge caused problems at extractions due to the higher chamber pressure.

Therefore the Hungarians started to develop their turn-bolt service rifle based on the Manlicher design to fire their 31M rimmed cartridge. This development resulted in the best Manlicher rifle, using the protruding Manlicher clip-loaded 5 round magazine, a two-piece stock, and a bolt handle that locked down ahead of the receiver bridge.

According to some photos the 35M Manlicher rifle had a sniper version, but no information that the troops ever got and used telescopically sighted rifles for sniping.

The 35M Manlicher service rifle weighted 4 kilograms unloaded; length 1110mm, barrel 600mm, muzzle velocity was 730m/sec.

In 1941 the deployed units of the Mobile Corps had no sub-machine guns. The paratroopers and the assault engineers were armed with German 35M Bergman 9mm sub-machine guns. The Hungarian war industry developed the 39M Király 9mm sub-machine gun, which was in the shape of a rifle, weighted 4,15kilogram. The 40-round detachable box magazine folds forward into a slot in the underside of the fore-end. 1566 were ordered from the Danuvia Factory in 1940, but the sub-machine guns did not arrive at the troops until 1943.

The standard squad light machine gun of the Hungarian Army was the 31M 8mm Solothurn light machine gun, produced under license in Hungary. The Swiss design weighted 9,5 kilogram and featuring a rapid barrel-change system introduced to facilitate prolonged firing from an air-cooled gun. However, the side-mounted 25-rounds curved box magazine only produced a rate of fire of 350 shots per minute. It had a bipod, in 1938 the mounting system was upgraded, got a solid tripod that able the 31M light machine gun to deliver more precise fire and used for platoon/company level A/A weapon too.

The standard machine gun of the Hungarians was also inherited from the K. und K. Armee of WW1. The 8mm 07/31M Schwarzlose machine gun was the only machine gun employing the retarded blow-back system the gun was very heavy and solid and due to the blow-back mechanism a short barrel fitted with a flash hider. The machine gun was transported in two, barrel system and bipod, in firing position weighted 40 kilograms. In 1931 the machine gun was re-barrelled to fire the new 31M cartridges. The rate of fire was 400 shots per minute; the weapon was fed by a fabric belt of 250cartridges. The 07/31M Schwarzlose machine guns were produced in Hungary until 1944.

Infantry heavy weapons

The company-level anti-tank weapon was the 36M 20mm anti-tank rifle, produced in Hungary under license from Solothurn, Switzerland. It was recoil-operated to give semiautomatic fire and had a well-padded shoulder–piece above a rear monopod, a combination that managed to absorb much of the recoil force. The anti-tank rifle weighed 45 kilograms, has a muzzle velocity of 762 meters per second, the armor penetration was only 15-18mm at the range of 300 meters. The rate of fire was 30-35 shots per minute. It fired a base-fused armor-piercing shell. It was a powerful anti-tank weapon of the 1930s but was outdated by 1941. It was transported by the chart, horse pack, vehicles, even on the side car of the motor bicycle. The 38M Toldi light tank and 39M Csaba armored car were also armed with the same weapon.

The company-level light mortar of the Hungarian troops was the home design 39M 50mm light mortar, developed and produced by the FÉG Factory. It weighed 20 kilograms in firing position. The rate of fire was 22 shots per minute delivered a shell of 845 grams; the range was between 50-860 meters. The rifle companies' heavy weapon platoons had two 39M light mortars and two 36M anti-tank rifles.

During the war, the Army used several types of hand grenades and rifle grenades. The Hungarian industry produced the home-produced 31M, 36M Vécsey hand grenades and 38/AM flame grenades. The troops also used German sticks and egg grenades.

The Hungarians were satisfied with the performance of the Cr.32 and was no other possibility to acquire new and better fighter planes, the Hungarians purchased the Cr.42 fighter biplane This plane belonged to the 2/4 Fighter Squadron with the unit sign "Winged Arrow", it was capable to counter the early Soviet fighters in 1941. [P. Mujzer]

The battalion level medium mortar of the troops was the 81mm 36M mortar. It entered into service in 1936, later was modified as 36/39M mortar. The mortar was transported in three parts. It weighed 85 kilograms in firing position. The range of fire was 4300-6200 meters; the rate of fire was 20-25 shots per minute and delivered a 4,125-kilogram shell. It was the best battalion-level heavy weapon of the troops.

The Hungarians used the 36M 37mm anti-tank guns, purchased from Germany. The design and development dated the back to late 20s. It was a very modern design for the period and used a well-sloped shield, tubular split-trail legs, and a long slender barrel. The gun was produced with spoked wheels for horse traction and steel wheels and pneumatic tires for vehicle traction. At the Hungarian Army, the motorized version was towed by Krupp Protze light artillery tractor, the horsed version was drawn by two horses' gun limber. The gun weighed 328 kilograms in firing position. The muzzle velocity of the armor-piercing projectile was 760meter/second; the armor penetration of the 354gram AP round was 38mm from the distance of 360meter. However, by 1941 the 37mm anti-tank guns were inferior against the medium and heavy tanks. On the Eastern Front, the 36M anti-tank gun was able to knock out the T-26 and BT tanks and armored cars of the Red Army but was ineffective against heavier armored vehicles.

Artillery

The Hungarian artillery consisted of mountain, field, heavy, and anti-aircraft artillery transported by pack animals, horse-drawn, and motor vehicles.

Field Artillery

The field artillery of the Mobile Corps consisted of horsed and motorized artillery; the troops of the VIII Corps also used packed mountain guns too.

The 1st Cavalry Brigade had one horsed artillery battalion equipped with 18M 80mm light field guns. The second artillery battalion was a motorized one, with 37M 105mm light howitzers towed by 37M Hansa Lloyd half-tracked artillery tractors. The cavalry regiments' hussar gun batteries were equipped with 35M 75mm guns, the horse-drawn version of the 15M mountain gun.

The Motorised Rifle Brigades had two-two motorized light howitzer battalions equipped with 37M 105mm howitzers towed by 37M Hansa Lloyd artillery tractors.

The cavalry and motorized rifle brigades had one-one A/A batteries with 36M 40mm Bofors guns.

The VIII Corps' subordinated brigades' artillery units had their horse-drawn 100mm and 150mm 14M light and medium field howitzers, 75mm 15M mountain guns. All of them were WW1 designs with limited range and mobility.

The Corps and Operational Group level artillery had motorized medium howitzer battalions equipped with 150mm howitzers towed by ancient Italian Pavesi artillery tractors. The Carpathian Operational Group was significantly reinforced with motorized anti-aircraft battalions equipped with 29M 80mm and 36M 40mm Bofors guns towed by Pavesi tractors and Ford Marmon trucks.

Anti-Aircraft Artillery

The Hungarians produced under license the 80mm 29 or 29/38M Bofors anti-aircraft gun from Sweden in 1929. The guns are assigned to the gun batteries of the anti-aircraft battalions. Although the gun had good ballistic characteristics it was difficult and time-consuming to make it ready to fire. The Bofors guns were towed by 28M Pavesi and later KV-40 artillery tractors.

The MÁVAG Factory produced the Swedish Bofors canon under license as the 40mm 36M anti-aircraft autocannon from 1936. It was one of the best Hungarian weapons during the war. The cannon was primarily used as an anti-aircraft cannon, but during the first part of the war used as a stopgap anti-tank weapon, later used against land targets too. The Bofors cannons were towed by Hansa Lloyd half-tracked tractors, Ford-Marmon, or 38M Botond trucks.

Armored vehicles

The Hungarian Armoured Troops deployed to Ukraine with Italian-made CV.35 tankettes, it was classified by the Hungarians as 35M Fiat Ansaldo, home-produced 38M Toldi light tanks, and 39M and 40M Csaba armored cars.

The Hungarian military purchased 150 CV-35 tankettes from Italy and named them the 35M Ansaldo. The armament of the Ansaldo was modified to one twin 34M 8mm Gebauer machine gun. The Hungarians invented an observer cupola, which was installed above the machine gunner's seat; each platoon and company commander's vehicle got this cupola. In the beginning, the tankettes were organized into automobile companies later into tankette companies subordinated to mixed brigades. Later the tankettes were regrouped into the reconnaissance and armored cavalry battalions. The bicycle battalions also got one-one tankette platoons. By the time of the operation, the tankettes were outdated.

The Swedish L-60 Landsverk was introduced in Hungary in 1937. The MAVAG Company, supported by the Ministry of Defence, purchased a sample and ran it through a series of competitive trials with the Weis Manfred Company's test vehicle. The Swedish tank was designated the 38M Toldi I light tank. The Ministry of Defence ordered 40 tanks from each company in February 1939. The Toldi light tank was almost 100% the same as the original L-60 except for the armament. Based on the opinion of the Military Technical Institute (HTI), the 20mm 36M anti-tank rifle with one 8mm 34/37A M co-axial machine gun was adopted for the Toldi tanks. After the first 80 vehicles, the Ministry of Defence ordered a second series of tanks which were designated the Toldi II due to some slight modifications. This meant that the Toldi became a 100% home-produced vehicle in 1940. The MAVAG Company began producing the German Bussing NAG engine, the Ganz Company produced the transmission, and the Ruggyantagyár Company manufactured the rubber wheel rims. In 1941, the 38M Toldi light tanks were suitable for reconnaissance and liaison duties only. The light tanks were fast and maneuverable, but lightly armed and armored.

In 1933 Mike Straussler, a former Hungarian engineer, designed a new four-wheel-drive armored car for the British Army and asked the Weiss Manfred Factory to produce the prototype for him. The AC I was manufactured in 1934; a new vehicle was designed in 1935. The AC II was a true military armored car with one front and one rear driving seat, and compartments, which were important on a reconnaissance mission. The Weiss Company produced two prototypes, one of which was for the British Army. The other remained at the factory.

In 1939 the Ministry of Defence ordered an armored car based on the design of Nicholas Straussler model designated the 39M Csaba, for the reconnaissance units. The hull and turret of the vehicle were designed jointly by Manfred Weiss and the HTI. It had an ideal shape, the armor plating being situated obliquely on the vehicle for added protection against bullets. The vehicle had one 20mm anti-tank rifle and one 8mm machine gun in the front of the turret, and one 8mm light machinegun was located to fire through the open rear turret hatch as an anti-aircraft weapon. In 1939 the Ministry of Defence ordered sixty-one 39M armored cars and delivered by Weiss Manfred Factory in 1940. The Army also ordered special command vehicles, the Csaba 40M, for the reconnaissance units, which had a greater radio capacity. The main requirement for this model was for it to be very similar to the combat vehicle, to keep production simple, and to avoid drawing special enemy attention to it. The command vehicle received a smaller turret with only one 8mm machine-gun, and a special frame radio mast. Only a dozen were built officially, though it is likely that a few damaged 39M were converted to command vehicles during the war.

The 39M and 40M Csaba armored cars and command/signal cars were up to the standards of the light armored cars at the beginning of the war.

Motor vehicles

Mechanization was one of the most important development projects for the Army. In the early years following WWI, financial difficulties created the main obstacle to mechanizing the Hungarian Army. During WWII the purchase of vehicles from abroad was also problematic. From 1928 to 1944 the Hungarian Army operated 160 different types of trucks and 24 types of motorbikes. The Army also used mobilized civilian vehicles, which made maintenance work difficult, if not impossible. Civilians whose trucks were commandeered by the Army for use in wartime received certain benefits. The owners were compensated for subsequently lost or damaged vehicles.

Home production

The backbone of the Hungarian automobile production based on the Magyar Wagon és Gépgyár (Rába) at Győr, the MÁVAG Factory at Budapest and the Weis Manfred Factory at Csepel.

The Weiss Manfred Factory developed the 1.5 tones WM-H1 6X4 truck in 1930. The Factory manufactured 54 modified WM-H2 trucks. Its technical solutions were later utilized during the development of the 38M Botond truck. Later the WM Factory produced was produced under license 178 Italian 28M Pavesi artillery tractors.

Magyar Wagon és Gépgyár (Rába) was the largest truck supplier to the Hungarian Army. In the early 1930s Rába produced 35 x 31M Rába-Krupp (3t) and 15 x 32M (4t) trucks.

Rába manufactured 350 Rába AFI 1.5 ton, 1635 Rába-Super 2.5 ton and 850 Rába-Special 3.5 ton trucks before the war.

The Hungarian Military Industry influenced by the Army started to develop its homemade all-terrain military truck using the developments of the WM-H 6x4 truck. The production was done in cooperation among the Magyar Waggon- és Gépgyár (Rába), MÁVAG, Weiss Manfred, Láng, Hofherr and Uhry Factories.

The 38M Botond had a four-stroke; four-cylinder 65 hp petrol engine with maximum speed 60 km/hours, range 300-400 kilometer, the truck transported 13 riflemen plus one driver. The 42M Botond got a stronger, 70 hp petrol engine. The first series of 1402 Botond trucks produced from 1938 until 1940 with a right-hand drive system.

The 38M Botond was among the best cross-country military trucks during WWII. It was used as a squad carrier for motorized rifles, for towing heavy weapons from PAK36 up to PAK40, 36M Bofors cannon, and even sometimes for towing 105mm howitzers.

The short-range reconnaissance squadrons were equipped with home-produced Weiss Manfred WM-21 and German Heinkel He 46 aircraft. This He 46 plane, F.328 belonged to the III Short-Range Reconnaissance Squadron. The aircraft had the yellow-painted engine and stripe on the fuselage; identification of Axis planes during the Yugoslavian Campaign. [War Correspondent Company]

Foreign vehicles

The Hungarians also purchased a significant number of vehicles from abroad, from Italy and Germany to equip the motorized units.

Already in 1932, the Hungarians acquired 104 Italian 32M Breda heavy artillery tractors. From 1938 until 1944, 800 trucks and cars of Italian origin were delivered to Hungary; among them were 100 6M Autocaretta-32 small all-terrain trucks, 38 Fiat-Spa Dovunque 2,5 tonnes trucks for Air Defence, 35 Fiat-Spa workshop trucks.

From Germany 2000 trucks and 1000 all-terrain command/staff vehicles were purchased between 1937-1940, among the delivered types were 240 38M Mercedes G5, 20 40M Horch-901 staff cars, 72 37M Krupp Protze large command car, 72 37M Krupp Protze L2H143 anti-tank gun towing vehicle, 74 37M Hansa Lloyd half-tracked artillery tractor, 355 37M Krupp Protze L2H143 half-squad carrier and 1099 39M Ford-Marmon trucks.

In 1941, the Germans handed over enough 2,5 tonne Ford BB chassis to the Hungarians to furnish 386 ambulance trucks, 431 special loaders, 200 fuel trucks with Hungarian Uhry-made superstructures.

In 1938 the Hungarians purchased 1000 2.5 t trucks from the USA, and 785 from Germany. These trucks were put into service as 38M Ford 2.5 tone truck, did not have 4-wheel drive. The Hungarians purchased the Marmon Herington license to rebuild the Ford as four-wheel-drive vehicles.

In 1939-40, under the Marmon-Herington license, 820 Ford trucks were rebuilt as four-wheel drive trucks as 39M Ford-Marmon 2.5 tone trucks. These were used to tow the 40mm Bofors A/A guns.

Artillery Tractors

From 1928 to 1932, 106 Pavesi tractors were purchased by the Army, and Manfred Weiss produced an additional 100 tractors, WM-Pavesi P4-100 (licensed by FIAT) put into service as 28M FIAT-Pavesi P4-100 artillery tractor. The vehicle was outclassed and unpopular, but due to the lack of other tractors, it remained in service until the end of WWII.

The 32M Breda heavy artillery tractor was also an outclassed WWI-style type, but 104 were purchased for use by the heavy artillery as towing vehicles for the 210mm howitzers and 305mm mortars. They remained in service until the end of the war.

In 1938-39 the Hungarian s purchased 74 Hansa-Lloyd Sd.Kfz.11 half-tracked artillery tractors, named as 37M Hansa-Lloyd half-tracked light artillery tractors to equip the 14 light howitzers and 4 Bofors A/A batteries, which were subordinated to the motorized rifle and cavalry brigades and bicycle battalions.

The H.S.C.S. K-40, K-50 artillery tractor originally agricultural tractor was entirely designed and made in Hungary. A military version was planned to tow the medium artillery and A/A guns. Up to 1942, 501 KV-40 were handed over to the Army. Later 60 more modern KV-50 were produced for the Army.

Motorcycles

The Hungarians used various civilian and military motorcycles for dispatch riders, movement control, reconnaissance duties, and at the motorcycle rifle companies serving at the reconnaissance and bicycle battalions. The side-car motorcycles were armed with light machine guns and 36M anti-tank rifles on special mountings.

Until 1940, the Hungarians purchased 4000-4000 German Puch 350G and Italian Gillera solo motor bicycles.

During the Barbarossa Campaign, in 1941 the motorcycle rifle companies were mostly equipped with mobilized civilian motorcycles, BMW R-75, Zündapp 597c, CWS Sokol M-111 (Polish) side-car, and Puch G350, CZ 175, Zündapp DB200W, Ariel, and Gilera solo motorbikes. These various civilian motorcycles were in bad mechanical condition, which meant that within a short time the motorcycle companies found themselves on foot during the battle. Nevertheless, the BMW and Zündapp motorbikes had proven themselves in difficult terrain and weather conditions. In the later stage of the war, the Hungarians focused on these types to acquire.

Captured vehicles in Hungarian service

An interesting episode of the Hungarian Army motorization was the Polish connection in 1939. Due to the military defeat of the Polish Army, about 70-80000 mostly military personals and their relatives had taken refuge in Hungary from mid-September until the early days of October. The Polish troops brought their weapons and equipment too. The 10th Polish Motorised Cavalry Brigade arrived with 600-800 trucks, 12-15 TKS tankettes, and artillery. According to international law, the Polish military personal were disarmed and interned. The confiscated Polish weapons, vehicles, and military equipment were taken over by the Hungarian Army. The most prized items were the Polish trucks and motorcycles. In 1938 the Hungarian Army had just 5200 motor vehicles, from civilian life about 3700 trucks and cars could be mobilized. In case of full mobilization, the Army needed 12000 motor vehicles to implement the existing 5200. Based on the Hungarian – Polish agreement, the confiscated Polish weaponry was incorporated into the Hungarian Army. The Polish motor vehicles arrived worn down, without spare parts and tool kits. The vehicles were repaired with the help of the Polish mechanics. In 1940, the Polish trucks, motorcycles constituted 15-20% of the vehicles of the Hungarian Army. During the first two years of the war, the Polish vehicles were used intensively by the mechanized units.

Hungarian Army in 1941

The manpower strength of the Hungarian Army in case of full mobilization was 450.000 men. Due to an extensive, mostly numerical, enlargement in May 1941 the Hungarian Army had 9 corps organized under 3 army commands plus the Mobile Corps and the AA Artillery Corps, 1-1 aviation and River forces brigades.

In detail, the peacetime organization and structure of the Hungarian Army consisted of 27 infantry, 4 cavalry regiments, 16 border guard, 9 bicycle, 6 motorized rifle 4 mountain jager, 2 reconnaissance, 2 armored cavalry, 2 light tank battalions. The artillery had 97 field, 6 horsed artillery, and 28 motorized artillery batteries. Among the motorized artillery were 5 heavy artillery battalions with 13 heavy batteries. The air defense artillery had 43 batteries, of which 24 were equipped with 80mm AA guns.

The Royal Hungarian Air Force had 2 fighter, 2 bomber, 1 short-range reconnaissance regiments, 1 long-range reconnaissance group, and 1 paratrooper battalion.

The River Forces consisted of 1-1 gunboat and minelayer/River obstacle regiments.

The Mobile Corps which were to be deployed to Ukraine was the most modern unit of the Hungarian Army with 2-2 motorized rifle and cavalry brigades at the out brake of the WW2.

Following the modernization and mechanization of the Hungarian Army; the Hungarian military leadership followed the foreign, German, Italian, Soviet military theories concerning the development, organization, and deployment of mechanized warfare. The first mechanized unit of the Hungarian Army, the Experimental Motorised Group, was established in 1932. It comprised of one motorized rifle company, a light tank, and an armored car company, two mechanized artillery batteries, and one motorcycle platoon.

After the commencement of the re-armament program, the Chief of the General Staff established the Mobile Branch with two cavalry brigades and one motorized rifle brigade, in the spring of 1938. The 2nd Motorised Rifle Brigade was based on the Experimental Motorised Group. It consisted of three motorized rifle battalions, two cyclist battalions, one mechanized artillery battalion, one reconnaissance battalion, one-one sapper and signal companies, and one A/A artillery battery.

In October 1938 another motorized rifle brigade, the 1st Motorised rifle Brigade was established with the same strength and organization as the 2nd

The elite light infantry troops of the Hungarian Army, the grenadier companies and jäger battalions, and the Experimental Motorised Group, were converted into motorized rifle battalions to provide the motorized rifle elements of the 1st and 2nd Motorised Rifle Brigades at the end of 1938.

The Mobile Corps was a complicated and complex unit, consisted of different kinds of units; motorized rifle, bicycle, cavalry, reconnaissance, bicycle-light tank battalions, supported by motorized, horsed artillery battalions and sapper, signal and supply troops. The Mobile Corps had 6-6 motorized rifle, bicycle, and cavalry battalions. The armored element consisted of 2-2 reconnaissance, bicycle-light tank, and armored cavalry battalions.

Casus Belli

When the Germans had begun preparing for the Barbarossa Campaign, they had not intended to involve Hungary as a fighting participant in the war against the Soviet Union. The German planners were skeptical of the fighting abilities and spirit of their allies on the south front. General Franz Hadler pointed out that" *It would be pointless to base our operational plans on forces which cannot be counted on with certainty. As far as actual fighting troops are concerned, we can depend only on German forces...In Romania, we cannot rely at all. Their divisions have no offensive power ... Hungary is unreliable. Has no reason s for turning on Russia."*

On the other hand, the Hungarian military leadership was informed unofficially; the Germans recommended the Hungarians to strengthen their border line adjacent to the Soviets. Even more, some kind of intelligence co-operation existed between the Hungarians and Germans. From the spring of 1941 unmarked German spy planes flown missions covertly over Soviet territories, taken off from Hungarian airfields. The Hungarian Junkers Junkers Ju-86 and Heinkel He-111 photo reconnaissance planes also flew high altitude sorties on demand of the Germans over the Carpathian Mountains.

When the war broke out between Germany and the Soviet Union, the Hungarians closed the Hungarian-Soviet border, activated the border defense system, and reinforced the frontier guard and air defense troops.

Within the Hungarian government were two interest groups advocating different attitudes towards the inevitable war against the Soviet Union. The senior military leadership, represented by the Chief of Staff of the Army, Colonel-General Henrik Werth was a strong supporter of the Hungarian involvement in the war from the beginning.

His explanation is based on the fact, that the Third Reich masterly blackmailed and manipulated its allies against each other to get more benefits and supports from them. Romania fully dedicated itself to the German war efforts not just providing staging areas, oil resources but deploying almost the entire Romanian Army on the Eastern Front. Nevertheless, strong Romanian units garrisoned at South-Transylvania facing the Hungarian troops in North-Transylvania. According to General Henrik Werth's explanation, if the Hungarians would not voluntarily join the Barbarossa Campaign it could have a negative consequence at the end of the war when the Third Reich would reward its loyal allies and punish the less dedicated once.

The Germans secretly also promised the Romanians to think over the territorial losses suffered by the arbitration of Germany and Italy in the favour of Hungary.

Some of the politicians and a few generals were less supportive of the German case and knew better the geopolitical realities of the war. They wanted to delay

The Hungarian Air Force had Junkers Ju 86K-2 and Caproni Ca.135bis medium bomber planes in 1941. These Ju 86K-2 bombers flying in V formations belonged to the 3/2 later 4/2 Bomber Squadron based at Tapolca airfield. [Fortepan/Erky-Nagy]

The Hungarians got some Heinkel He 111P-2/P-4 long-range reconnaissance version of the Heinkel He 111 bomber planes. This plane stationed at the airfield of Pécs has the B.702 code which was changed to F. soon. The Hungarian Heinkel planes made long-range sorties over Ukraine in 1941. [Fortepan/Varga dr]

and minimize the Hungarian military involvement. They tried to keep a fair connection with the western allies as well as with the Soviet Union. The leading figure of this approach was Prime Minister Pál Teleki, who committed suicide, upon realizing that his intention to keep Hungary out of the war failed in April of 1941. His successor, László Bárdosy, was less well connected and influential than his predecessor. Governor Miklós Horty, an ardent anti-communist, was in crossfire of his ministers and generals, hesitating what to do.

Furthermore, the Hungarian society similarly to other nations were deeply impressed by the successful "Blitzkrieg" of the Germans performed in 1939-1941.

At 1240hrs on 26 June, Soviet Polikarpov I-16 fighters strafed an express train traveling from Kőrösmező to Budapest, killing one civilian and wounding several others. Half an hour later, three unidentified aircraft attacked the Hungarian town of Kassa (modern-day Košice, Slovakia), killing 32 people and wounding more than 110.

Kassa was a garrison town of the Hungarian VIII Corps and some of its subordinates as well as for reconnaissance and motorized rifle battalions of the 2nd Motorised Rifle Brigade. The Aviation Academy of the Royal Hungarian Air Force is also based in the town and the airfield. Surprisingly military targets were lightly hit, but the Main Post Office and residential areas were severely damaged.

The anti-aircraft and early warning units were unable to identify the nationality of the attacking planes. No military insignia was observed on the bomber planes. The investigation, based on the splinters and one unexploded bomb, later concluded that the air attack was carried out by the Red Air Force.

Of course, the Soviets denied their involvement in the attack on Kassa. From the beginning, different conspiracy theories spread among the Hungarians. The well-accepted theories were; that the Germans were behind the action to involve Hungary in the Barbarossa or that Romania did it on behalf of the Germans or acted independently to push their rivals into the war. However, most likely three Soviet SB-2 bomber planes committed the air raid. It happened on the fourth day of the war when the Red Air force wanted to stop or at least slow down the attackers on all fronts. The inexperienced Soviet air crew just had very limited navigation skills, where lack of proper and updated maps. Just three years ago, Kassa/Kosice belonged to Czechoslovakia, currently a hostile territory for the Soviet Forces. Most probably the Soviet bomber flight took off and flew towards the west to find a target big enough to bomb.

However, it was a perfect "casus belli" for Hungary's pro-German military leadership to involve the country in the war against the Soviet Union. Colonel-General Henrik Werth went to Horthy and reported before the proper investigation, that the bomb attack was carried out by Soviet planes. He cleverly appealed to the military honor and the anti-communism of Admiral Miklós Horthy. It was enough for the Governor to decide on the war at the Cabinet Meeting.

The following morning the Royal Hungarian Air Force attacked Soviet targets in Ukraine, and Hungary and the Soviet Union were at war.

Opposing Forces, the Red Army

The Kiev Military District, under the leadership of Colonel-General Kirponos, defended the 940km long border with 907.000 men. Upon the mobilization, the Southwest Front was on the main axis of attack by the German Army Group South during Operation Barbarossa. The Southern Front commanded by General Tyulenev was mobilized on the Odessa Military District was also facing the German Army Group South.

Junkers Ju 86K-2 bomber plane of the 3/1 later 4/1 Bomber Squadron and Heinkel He 70K long-range reconnaissance planes of the 1st Long Range Reconnaissance Group parking at the airfield of Kecskemét. ([Fortepan/Hidvégi]

The Hungarian purchased 18 Heinkel He 70K long-range reconnaissance planes from Germany with Hungarian produced engine, to equip the 1st Long Range Reconnaissance Group. The unit was based at the airfield of Kecskemét in 1941. [Fortepan/Hidvégi]

At the outbreak of war with Germany, the Southwest Front contained the Soviet 5th, 6th, 26th, and 12th Armies along the frontier. 16th and 19th Armies were in reserve behind the forward forces. Three of its four armies and four of its eight mechanized corps of the Southwest Front were concentrated to defend the Lvov salient.

The Southwest Front consisted of 11 Rifle Corps (32 Rifle and Mountain Rifle Divisions), 8 Mechanised Corps (18 Tank and 8 Mechanised Divisions), 1 Cavalry Corps (2 Cavalry Divisions), 1 Airborne Corps (3 Airborne Brigades), and 4 Anti-Tank Brigades. The Front Air Forces had 2 Fighter Aviation Divisions, 2 Bomber

The Hungarian WM-21 Hawk short-range reconnaissance plane was developed from the Fokker X. aircraft and manufactured by the Weiss Manfred Factory, an already outdated model actively used in 1941 at the Eastern Front. [Fortepan/Marics]

The Hungarian River Forces were responsible for the protection of the main rivers of Hungary, basically the Danube and the Tisza, and supporting the land forces alongside these rivers. The Gunboat Regiment had modernized WW1 gunboats operating on the River Danube, smaller minesweepers operated on the River Tisza. Gunboats moor at the Elisabeth Bridge, Budapest 1927. [Fortepan/Göcseji Múzeum]

Aviation Divisions, 5 Mixed Aviation Divisions, and 2 Air Reconnaissance Regiments.

The Southern Front had the 9th Army and front units consisted of 5 Rifle Corps, 2 Mechanised, and 1-1 Cavalry and Airborne Corpses. The Black Sea Fleet also belonged to the Southern Front with its naval and naval aviation units. The air support numbered 3 Mixed Aviation Division and one –one Naval Fighter and Bomber Brigades.

The 12th Soviet Army was located on the Soviet-Hungarian border, from Borislav to Kamenyec-Podolszk. The 12th Army of the Soviet Red Army was formed from the Southern (Cavalry-Mechanised) Army Group of the Kiev Special Military District during 1939-40. It was then involved in the Soviet invasion of Poland in 1939.

Major General Pavel Grigoryevich Ponedelin (4 March 1893 – Moscow 25 August 1950) became commander of the 12th Army in March 1941. He was a Soviet general executed after World War II for being taken prisoner by the Germans.

The 12th Army entered the Second World War as part of the Soviet Southwest Front, consisted of:

13th Rifle Corps commanded by Major General Nikolay Kirillov

44th Mountain Rifle Division commanded Major General S. A. Tkachenko

58th Mountain Rifle Division commanded Major General N. I. Proshkin

192nd Mountain Rifle Division commanded Major General S. D. Gubin

17th Rifle Corps commanded Major General Ivan Galanin

60th Mountain Rifle Division commanded Major General M. B. Salikhov

96th Mountain Rifle Division commanded Colonel I. M. Shepetov

164th Rifle Division commanded Colonel A. N. Chervinskiy

16th Mechanised Corps commanded Major General Aleksandr Sokolov

15th Tank Division commanded Colonel V. I. Polozkov

39th Tank Division commanded Colonel N. V. Starkov

240th Mechanised Division commanded Colonel I. V. Gorbenko

19th Motorcycle Regiment)

10th, 11th, and 12th Fortified Regions, and artillery, engineering, and other units.

The whole strength of the 12th Army was 6 rifle divisions, 5 of them were mountain rifle divisions, 2 tanks, and 1 mechanized division, 1 motorcycle regiment, 1 artillery brigade, 4 artillery regiments, the fortified regions each were equivalent to brigade size. However, just half of the Soviet infantry units faced the Hungarians, the other half committed against the German and Romanian forces. The 16th Mechanised Corps deployed in deep behind the first line.

In the Hungarian-Soviet border area, the Hungarian intelligence identified 10 rifles, 1 mountain rifle, 2 cavalry, and 3 mechanized divisions, which was an over calculation.

The actual Soviet troops facing the Hungarians were 58th and 192nd Mountain Divisions of the 13th Rifle Corps, and the 96th Mountain Division of the 17th Rifle Corps.

The backbone of the Red Army was the rifle divisions 196 that existed in 1941. The M39 Rifle Division had 18841 men; the M41 rifle division had a reduced strength of 14483 men.

The M39 division had an HQ, three rifle regiments, one-one light and medium artillery regiments (three 3-batteries battalions each), one-one reconnaissance, anti-aircraft, anti-tank, engineers, signal and medical battalions plus supply and support troops.

The rifle regiments had an HQ; anti-aircraft, infantry gun, anti-tank, mortar batteries, reconnaissance, engineer and signal companies, and three rifle battalions.

The rifle battalions had an anti-tank platoon, machine gun (12x Maxim M1910 heavy machine guns) and mortar companies, and three rifle companies. Each rifle company had a machine gun platoon (2x Maxim

The main armament of the gunboats positioned in the aft and bow turrets. The original twin 77mm short barrel guns were replaced by 80mm light guns. The sailors had a modern navy-style uniform, instead of blue, it was the khaki color. [P. Mujzer]

Lined up River Forces formation presenting arms during the celebration of the Battle of Otranto, a famous naval battle of WW1 led by Miklós Horthy, who becomes the governor of Hungary in 1920. The commemoration was held at the barracks of the River Forces at Óbuda (outskirt of Budapest). [Fortepan/Szabó]

M1910 heavy machine gun) and three rifle platoons, each with four 12 men rifle squads.

The M41 Rifle Division had reorganized HQ troops and the divisional artillery was upgraded from 3 to 5 battalions per artillery regiments.

The Red Army organized 19 Mountain Rifle Divisions, recruiting heavily from the Transcaucasian Military District. Uniquely, a 40M Mountain Rifle Division had four 5-companies mountain regiments omitting the intermediate battalion echelon. The troops were supplied with horsed and mule supply columns. However, the troops did not receive specific mountain training like the German and Hungarian mountain troops.

Facing the Hungarian troops the Soviet 12th Army had the 96th and 192nd Mountain Rifle Divisions.

An M41 Mechanised Division was 11.200 men strong and had an HQ with reconnaissance, anti-aircraft, anti-tank, and engineer battalions, one light tank regiment (5 tank battalions), one artillery regiment (3 artillery battalion), and two motor rifle regiment (3 rifle battalions each).

An M41 Tank Division was 11343 men strong and had an HQ with reconnaissance, anti-aircraft, anti-tank, signal, and engineer battalions, two tank regiments (3 tank battalion each), one artillery and one motor rifle regiments.

The cavalry was reorganized three times, from 1939 to 1941, finally, the M41 Cavalry Division had 9.240 men and consisted of HQ, signal, engineer, medical, chemical warfare, and supply companies. The three cavalry regiments were supported by one horsed artillery battalion and one tank company.

Pioneers in the development of airborne troops and tactics, the Soviets began parachuting small-scale units in the early 30s. Based on the positive experiences the Soviet Airborne Forces were expanded by 1941 into five Airborne Corps, each corps had three airborne brigades. An Airborne Brigade consisted of HQ, signal, reconnaissance, and mortar, anti-aircraft companies, 4 parachute battalions, one infantry gun, and two anti-tank gun batteries. However, the lack of suitable transport planes, the German air superiority rendered the airborne troops to fight as elite infantry.

Operation of the Carpathian Operational Group

Mobilization and deployment

On the Hungarian side, an operational group was formed on 30 June to carry out the military operation against the Red Army in Ukraine. It was called the "Carpathian Group" directly subordinated to the Chief of Staff of the Army, Colonel-General Henrik Werth. The Operational Group was led by Lieutenant General Ferenc Szombathelyi the commander of the VIII Corps. He was one of the most experienced Hungarian generals, also commanding the Ludovika Military Academy in 1936-1938, later appointed to be the Chief of Staff of the Hungarian Army from 1941 until 1944.

The Hungarian units fought under German command and Hungarian liaison teams were assigned to the German command structure to the Army Group South, to the German 11th and 17th German Army, as well as to the German 4th Luftflotte. The Hungarian liaison officers were in a delicate position to balance between the German demands and the Hungarian fighting capacity. At least the communication was not a problem, the Hungarian liaison officers were fluent German.

The Operational Group consisted of the VIII Corps, the Mobile Corps, and reinforcements.

The VIII Corps had 1st Mountain Brigade and 8th Frontier Guard Brigade and reinforcements. The 1st Mountain Brigade, commanded by Major General Jenő Felk had four mountain battalions, one mountain artillery battalions. The 8th Border Guard Battalion led by Major General György Rakovszky consisted of 6 border guard battalions and one border guard artillery battalion. The VIII Corps was reinforced with two bicycle battalions, six anti-aircraft artillery battalions, one field and one medium motorized artillery battalions, two sappers, and one railway construction battalions.

During the Ukrainian operation, the Mobile Corps led by Major General Béla Miklós and comprised of three brigades: the 1st and 2nd Motorised Rifle and 1st Cavalry Brigades, the 2nd Cavalry Brigade left home. The Mobile Corps reinforced with the I., V., VIII. Medium Artillery Battalions, the VI., VII. Bicycle Battalions, and the 152nd Engineer and 150th Signal Battalions.

On 26 June 1941 three unidentified two-engine bomber planes hit Kassa (Kosice). The unexpected air raid costs severe civilian casualties, but no military targets were hit. The building of the Main Post Office was hit by 150 kilograms bombs. The attack provided "caus belli" for the Hungarians entering the war. [Fortepan/Schermann]

The commander of the 1st Motorised Rifle Brigade was Major General Jenő Major, the 2nd Motorised Rifle Brigade was led by Major General János Vörös and the 1st Cavalry Brigade was commanded by Major General Antal Vattay.

The Mobile Corps was equipped with 508 light machine guns, 168 machine guns, 52 anti-tank rifles, 40 light mortars, 12 mortars, 80 anti-tank guns, 60 AA guns (80 and 40mm), and 90 field artillery pieces. The armored elements of the Mobile Corps had 81-87 light tanks, 48 armored cars, and 60 tankettes.

Hungarian mountain trooper manning an observation post at the border overlooking a road running in the valley. He is armed with a 31M light machine gun, his leather binocular case is on the parapet. He has a special cavalry waist belt with a leather strap to secure his carbine. [War Correspondent Company]

Hungarian mountain trooper climbing up on the peaks of the Carpathian Mountain, bypassing the valleys blocked by the Soviet forces. The Hungarian mountain troops were organized in 1939 to meet the demands of the mountain war due to the regain Carpathian regions. [War Correspondent Company]

Hungarian mountain trooper climbing with rope, armed with 8mm 35M rifle equipped with special rucksack designed for mountainous operations. The mountain troops had a visor hat version of the traditional "Bocskai" field cap. [War Correspondent Company]

Aviation Group supported the ground forces with fighter, bomber, and short-range reconnaissance squadrons. Equipped with Fiat CR.42 fighters, Junkers Ju-86K-2 bombers, He-46, and WM-21short-range reconnaissance planes. During the operation Reggiane Re.2000 fighters and Caproni Ca.135 bombers joined them.

The Mobile Corps had received its mobilization order at its peacetime garrisons on 26 June. It was ordered

Hungarian hussar patrol advancing in a creek, avoiding the few but congested roads in the Carpathians. The personal equipment of the mounted men carries by their horses. Extra ammunition pouches are attached to the saddle. [War Correspondent Company]

The withdrawing Soviet forces demolished bridges, tunnels, and culverts to slow down the advancing Axis troops. The Hungarians had limited engineer capacity to repair the destroyed objects. Advancing Hungarian sappers wore engineer half-boots and their engineer tools; spades, axes, saws attached to their backpacks. [War Correspondent Company]

Hungarian hussars watering their horses at a creek. The 35M cavalry sabres are still attached to the saddle, some of the horses carry the metal ammunition box for the squad 31M light machine gun. [War Correspondent Company]

Hussar platoon led by a 2nd lieutenant wearing a none issued trench coat, at the beginning of the operation the weather was rainy, complicated the life of the men on the field. The cavalry could move easier on difficult terrain than the motorized troops. [War Correspondent Company]

Hussar squadron of the 4th Hussar Regiment climbing on the mountain serpentine at Halajkovce. The cavalrymen lead their horses on foot, among the hussar horses are pack-horses loaded with 31M light machine guns. [Illésfalvi]

Hungarian pack animal supply column moving on a mountain pass at the Carpathian Mountains. Due to the destroyed road network, the advancing troops relied heavily on supply transported by pack animals. [War Correspondent Company]

The pack animals were led individually by their handlers, transporting ammunition, food, and equipment for the troops. But had limited capacity, in some cases, food and ammunition were air delivered by parachute drops to the troops. [War Correspondent Company]

Hungarian supply column of the 3rd Motorised Rifle Battalion crossing a makeshift bridge erected on the River Zbruch at Skala-Podilska. The 39 M Ford-Marmon trucks followed by a 38M Botond and a Krupp Protze trucks. In the background are staff cars, R/7 signal trucks, and Ford trucks visible. [Fortepan/Hajdú Fedő]

Demolished bridge on the River Zbruch. The Hungarian sappers could easily lay down wooden planks to make the bridge passable. The Red Army demolished more than 21 bridges during the retreat in the path of the Hungarian forces. [Fortepan/Hajdú Fedő]

to assemble ready for marching forward by 29 June. The mobilization was very slow and was not completed. At the time of moving out, its strength was only about 75-80%.

Under the new organization, the motorized rifle brigades had one light tank battalion and one reconnaissance battalion, and the cavalry brigade had one armored battalion. The 1st Motorised Rifle Brigade had the 9th Bicycle-Tank Battalion, and the 2nd Brigade had the 11th Bicycle-Tank Battalion. The battalions' title and organization reflected on their transitional state.

The bicycle-light tank battalions consisted of the battalion HQ (3 x 38M Toldi light tanks), sapper, signals, maintenance platoons, and the 1st and 2nd Bicycle Companies and 3rd and 4th Tank Companies (18-18 x 38M Toldi light tanks).

Motorised supply column of the 1st Armoured Cavalry Battalion crossing the River Zbruch on a makeshift bridge. The 38M Botond truck carries the unit sign on the left mudguard towing a field kitchen, called goulash canon, followed by requisitioned civilian cars and Ford-Marmon trucks. [War Correspondent Company]

Hungarian horse draw supply column marching in the valley the Tisza River to support the advancing troops of the Carpathian Operational Group. The mountain, frontier guard, and cavalry units had horse-drawn supply columns. Due to the congestion on the supply road, the resupplies of the troops were delayed. [NL-HANA]

Bicycle troops taking a short rest during the advance in the Carpathian Mountains, crossing the Carpathian Mountains was very demanding to the so-called "rubber hussars". Next to the bicycle troops 38M Toldi light tanks moving towards the front line. [P. Mujzer]

Demolished viaduct at Jaremce over the river Prut, the Hungarian 38M Botond trucks proceeding on the riverbank of Jaremce. The Hungarian engineer troops are already working on the destroyed road bridge. [Fortepan/Hajdú Fedő]

As of 1 July 1941, the 9th Bicycle- Tank Battalion equipment consisted of 39 x 38M Toldi light tanks, 52 trucks, 11 cars, 37 solo, 2 sidecar motorbikes, 2 ambulances, 1-1 signal, and a fuel truck. The bicycle companies had 206 bicycles/ company. Of course, the light tank and bicycle companies were deployed separately.

The 1st and 2nd Reconnaissance Battalions had one armored car company (16 x 39M Csaba armored cars), a motorized rifle company, a motorcycle company, and the battalion staff had one anti-tank platoon (four 37mm 36M anti-tank guns), one signal and one sapper platoon. The motorcycle companies were equipped with military and mobilized civilian motorcycles, BMW R-75, Zündapp 597c, CWS-MIII (Polish) sidecar, and Puch G350, CZ 175, Zundapp DB200W, Ariel, and Gilera.

The 1st Cavalry Armoured Battalion had one armored car company (16 x 39M Csabas armored cars), two tankette companies (9 x 38M Toldi light tanks, and 36 x 35M Fiat Ansaldo tankettes), and one anti-tank company with 37mm 36M anti-tank guns. The battalion staff had one-one signal, sapper, and maintenance platoons. Each tankette company had three tankette platoons (six 35M Ansaldo tankettes each), and one light tank platoon (four 38M Toldi light tank). The remaining 38M Toldi light tank served at the battalion staff.

The most complicated unit of the Mobile Corps were the bicycle battalions, each consisted of three bicycle companies (12 x 31M LMG and 2 x 36M anti-tank rifle each), one motorized heavy weapon company (6 x 07/31M HMG), battalion staff with one-one sapper, signal, maintenance, anti-tank (4 x 36M anti-tank gun) and tankette platoons. The bicycle battalions also had one motorized light field howitzer battery equipped with 4 x 37M 105mm howitzers and 37M Hansa Lloyd

Troops of the 1st Armoured Cavalry Battalion waiting at Jaremce, the 35M Fiat Ansaldo tankettes and the Ford truck belonged to the tankette companies of the battalion. The tankett companies lost a significant number of Ansaldo tankettes due to the deployment without contacting the enemy. [Fortepan/Hajdú Fedő]

Crew of the 35M Fiat Ansaldo tankett wearing a crash helmet and canvas mechanics overall. By that time the tankettes were severely outdated with their twin 8mm 34MA machine guns, weak armor, and underpowered engines. [War Correspondent Company]

Hungarian sappers repairing a demolished culvert to provide safe passage for the Hungarian motor vehicles at the Carpathian Mountain. These kinds of obstacles slowed down the advance of the Hungarian troops in the early stage of the war. [War Correspondent Company]

half-tracked artillery tractors. The four bicycle battalions, 10th, 12th, 13th, 14th tankette platoons' had six 35M Fiat Ansaldo tankettes, for a total of 24.

The total strength of the Carpathian Operational Group was about 93000 men, 3355 officers, 89760 men, 21265 horses, 3308 horse-drawn wagons, and 5858 motor vehicles. The combat units consisted of 33 battalions, 17 artillery battalions. In detail, it had 8 bicycles, 6-6 motorized and border guard, 4 mountain jager, 2-2 light tank and reconnaissance, 1 armored cavalry battalions, and 2 cavalry regiments. The troops were supported by 2 motorized medium howitzer, 3 motorized light howitzer, 1-1 horsed, field and mountain artillery, 8 anti-aircraft artillery battalions, and 4 Bofors batteries. The support units consisted of 3 sapper, 1 signal, and 1 railway construction battalions.

Hungarian bicycle troops climbing up in the Carpathian Mountain through the Tatarovo Pass, pushing their heavy military bicycles in front of the border guard post of Uzhgorod. The flag hung over the building with HIR meant for the signal station. [Mujzer]

Hungarian troopers of the Motorcycle Rifle Company of the 2nd Reconnaissance Battalion commanded by Captain Zoltán Örményi, pushing their Sokol M-111 sidecar motorbikes on the railway tracks at the Tatar Pass. The troops dressed in greatcoats and half poncho due to the pouring rain. [War Correspondent Company]

Ex-Polish Sokol M-111 sidecar motorbike fording the Zbruch River also belonged to the 2nd Reconnaissance Battalion. The troopers wearing Italian-style crash helmets. One 38M Botond truck and a staff car assembled on the river bank. [War Correspondent Company]

Initial operations

The Hungarian VIII Corps and the subordinated units were alerted on 18 June to be prepared to occupy the border defense positions alongside the Hungarian-Soviet border. When the German offensive started the Hungarian troops went in a defensive position along the borderline to monitor the Soviet side of the border.

According to the Hungarian reconnaissance reports, the Soviet border guard units occupied the defensive position alongside the Soviet-Hungarian border from 22 June. The Hungarians observed that the Soviet troops took defensive preparations, tunnels,

The northern bridgehead of the destroyed railway viaduct at the River Jaremce. The Hungarian railway construction units worked hard to restore the traffic. The photo was taken from the already rebuilt road bridge by Ensign Berkó, supply officer of the 150th Military Bridge Column. [Fortepan/Berkó]

The advancing Hungarian troops were significantly reinforced with motorized anti-aircraft artillery battalions armed with 29M 80mm Bofors guns. The guns were towed by the Hungarian KV-40 artillery tractor with noisy, underpowered diesel engines unable to negotiate the mountainous terrain. [War Correspondent Company]

The 101st Armoured Train was deployed to reconnoiter the railway lines until the old Soviet frontier. Due to the different gauge scale of the European and the Russian railways, the Hungarian armored train was deployed until the end of the East-Poland border. The 101st Armoured Train had chevron-style military insignia stationed at the Railway Station of Körösmező. [HIM]

Hungarian 80mm 29M Bofors was stuck in the mud during the advance in the Carpathian Mountains. The crew tries to extract the cumbersome gun. It was an effective artillery piece, but difficult to transport and made it ready to fire. [War Correspondent Company]

The river crossing is protected by a 40mm 36M Bofors anti-aircraft autocannon. The Bofors cannons could operate independently against air targets because issued with range finders and calculators attached to the cannons. The gunner in the centre wearing the old 17M steel helmet, the others issued with the 35M helmets. [HaNa]

Engine test of the Fiat Cr.42 biplane fighter. In 1941, the Italian Fiat Cr.42 biplane fighters were the backbone of the Hungarian fighter squadrons deployed to the front line. Slow, but manoeuvrable fighters with the trained crew were credible opponents of Soviet fighters. [Fortepan/Varga]

Damaged Fiat Cr.42 fighter plane with local children and maintenance crew. The fighter plane emergency landed nearby a village and repaired on the ground. The plane had the red-white-green chevron military insignia painted on the wing. [Fortepan/Kerekes]

The Ground element of the III Short Range Reconnaissance Squadron deployed by train through the Carpathian Mountains closer to the operational area. The Squadron was equipped with Hungarian-made WM-21 Hawk aircraft. [Fortepan/Varga dr.]

Troops of the 15th Bicycle Battalion deployed by train towards the assembly area, the air defense provided by an 8mm 07/31M Schwarzlose machine gun on an AA tripod. The next train belonged to a German unit, the unit sign; white leaping deer is visible on the truck. [Fortepan/Csorba]

bridges prepared for demolition; at Beskids Pass, a rail bridge was dismantled.

The commander of the 8th Frontier Guard Brigade, Major General Rakovsszky tasked a reinforced mountain jager half-company to be prepared to capture the railway tunnel at the Beskids in case of hostilities.

The hostilities already started on 27 June, on a low, tactical level, both sides send out patrols to probe the enemy along the passable roads around the Tatarov and Verecke Passes. The 12th Soviet Army reported only minor skirmishes with the Hungarian mountain jagers.

The first goal of the Carpathian Operational Group was to capture the area of Zaleshchiki – Kolomea-Stanislav. The units of the VIII Corps were tasked to clear the passes of the northeaster Carpathian Mountains and captured the towns of Deliatyn, Nadworna, Dolina, and Skole on the highland. After that, the motorized units of the Mobile Corps could be deployed through the cleared mountain roads and passes to advance into the region lying south of the River Dniester, southern Galicia.

The successful German operation at Lvov meant that the Hungarians had to move quickly to keep up with the advancing German forces. The task of the Hungarian

39M Csaba armored car belonged to the Armoured Car Company of the 2nd Armoured Cavalry Battalion crossing the River Pruth on a temporary bridge next to the demolished one. The 2nd Armoured Cavalry Battalion was not deployed as a whole unit to the front, but its armored car and anti-tank gun companies were subordinated to the Carpathian Operational Group during the first phase of the operation. [Móker]

3rd Light Tank Company of the 9th Bicycle -Light Tank Company Battalion waiting for the marching order at the street of Kolomea surrounded by local civilians, Hungarian and Ukrainian flags can be seen on the buildings. [War Correspondent Company]

Hungarian 38M light tank advancing among the ruined buildings of Kolomea during the capture of the town. The town was hit by the bombers of the Luftwaffe and the Royal Hungarian Air Force. [War Correspondent Company]

38M Toldi light tanks of the 4th Light Tank Company / 9th Bicycle – Light Tank Battalion advancing towards Kamenec-Podol'skyi. Hungarian trucks and cars hide alongside the road under the trees to avoid the Red Air Force's attention. [NL-HANA]

forces was to maintain the connection between the 17th German Army and the 3rd Romanian and 11th German Armies and to pursue the withdrawing Red Army units.

The Carpathian Group began its advance with its border guard and mountain troops on the lead on the morning of 28 June, through very difficult mountainous terrain. At 10.30 hours the Hungarian 1st Mountain Battalion reported that the Soviet troops withdrawing at the Beskids, and preparing for demolition of the Railway Station and tunnel of Beskids. According to the plan a reinforced mountain half-company charged and captured the tunnel of Beskids. The mountain advanced

Hungarian officers sightseeing at Kamenec-Podol'skyi. The buildings of this Eastern-Poland town were built during the Habsburg Monarchy, rather worn down but a familiar sight for the older Hungarian officers. [Fortepan/Berkó]

Destroyed houses at Kamenec-Podol'skyi, Polish Market Square. The town was bombed by the German Luftwaffe and the Royal Hungarian Air Force before the Hungarians occupied it. The Hungarian officers calmly walk on the street. [Fortepan/Berkó]

Staged photo, a Hungarian soldier wearing its 35M steel helmet is in a firing position with his 8mm 31M Manlicher rifle with fixed bayonet at the old fort of Kamenec-Podol'skyi. [War Correspondent Company]

Troopers of the 15th Bicycle Battalion entering into the old city of Kamenec-Podol'skyi through the half-demolished viaduct. The bicycle troops carried their equipment and weapons on their 32M military bicycle. On the left is a broken Hungarian civilian bus mobilized by the Army, used for medical or staff duties. [War Correspondent Company]

at 12.00 hours and within 30 minutes they overpowered the Soviet troops and occupied the railway tunnel intact passing under the borderline and occupied Beskids. The 8th Border Guard Brigade was able to hold these vital positions against several Soviet counter-attacks. The intact tunnel was vital to deploy the Hungarian Armoured Train 101st for reconnaissance of the railway lines on the Soviet side of the border. The first Hungarian soldiers killed in action were Lance Corporal Sándor Tóvízi and Private József Torzsás, both belonged to the 25th Border Guard Battalion.

The next day, the advancing Hungarian advance guards collide into a Soviet motorized rifle unit reinforced with armored cars. During the protracted clashes,

Hungarian sappers repairing the demolished bridge at Kamenec-Podol'skyi. The soldier on the left is armed with an 8mm 35M Manlicher rifle with a long 35M bayonet. The tin rooftops were torn apart by the blast of aerial bombs. [War Correspondent Company]

Hungarians stopped the Soviet troops, but they were overnumbered and withdrawn to the main force. The Hungarian 36M (Pak 36) anti-tank guns knocked out some Soviet BA armored cars and one was captured intact.

The 1st Mountain Brigade's troops secured the heights commanding the Tatarov Pass and provided safe roads to their troops advancing through the valleys below.

The Soviet forces put up fierce resistance in regimental size infantry groups reinforces with artillery and mortars. The upper Pruth Valley was blocked by deep and wide mine belts. The only road of the advancing Hungarian troos, Körösmező-Tatarov-Deliatyn road was severely damaged by blowing up the bridges, railway lines even culverts 40-50 km depth into the Soviet territory from the border.

Within the Carpathian Mountains, the Soviet engineers destroyed 21 bridges, tunnels, and the rivers in flood also complicated the operations. However, not all of the bridges were properly demolished, sometimes just one part of the bridges blown up, which made it easy to rebuild.

1-2 July 1941 the Hungarian began to move through the Carpathian mountain passes, chasing the units of the 58th Mountain Rifle Division/Southwest Front withdrawing from the border and fighting for the passes.

Abandoned Soviet BT-7A artillery tank armed with 76,2mm howitzer in a captured Galician town surrounded by civilians and Hungarian soldiers. The officer on the right wearing mountain boots, the officer in the middle had a visor hat field cap. [P. Mujzer]

38M Toldi light tanks of the 1st Armoured Cavalry Battalion bypassing a Hungarian hussar squadron resting at the roadside. The unit sign of the 1st Armoured Cavalry Battalion is painted on the back left side of the light tank. The tankette companies were reinforced with one-one light tank platoons equipped with 38M Toldi light tanks. [Illésfalvi]

Hungarian Hussars wading through a flooded river in the Carpathian Mountain. In difficult terrain, the cavalry had better mobility than the motorized troops. Contrary to the summer the weather was quiet chili in the Carpathian Mountains. [War Correspondent Company]

The tin-roofed buildings were typical in Galicia. In Kamenec-Podol'skyi the blast of the bombs simply removed the roofs and destroyed the windows. [NL-HANA]

Town of Kamenec-Podol'skyi was hit by Axis air raids before the arrival of the Hungarian troops. The street is littered with the debris of the explosions, civilians are in the background trying to clean up the destroyed buildings. [NL-HANA]

Destroyed railway viaduct over the River Pruth, at Jaremce, it was difficult and take time to rebuild by the Hungarian engineers. To restore the railway lines was important to maintain the supply flow through the mountainous terrain. [Fortepan/Teller]

The Hungarians built a temporary wooden road bridge laid on the existing pillars of the blown-up bridge on the River Pruth. Another bridge pillars are visible next to the rebuilt one, it belonged to a demolished railway bridge. The wrecked bridge parts already cleared out of the riverbed. [Fortepan/Teller]

Hungarian supply column equipped with 37M Ford trucks crossing a small river in the Carpathians on a 33M military bridge. The heavy rains frequently washed away the temporary bridges. The 33M military bridge was a very modern piece of equipment; the bridge and support structure was made of light-weighted aluminum. [Fortepan/Berkó]

Hungarian Ford truck belonged to the 3rd Motorised Rifle Battalion turned into the river from a makeshift wooden plank bridge at the Carpathian Mountains. The troops prepare to recover the vehicle with the help of a 38M Botond truck. [Fortepan/Hajdú Fedő]

Ambushed Krupp Protze truck of the Heavy Weapon Company of the 3rd Motorised Rifle Battalion. Possible hit by a small-caliber mortar round at the engine and shot by small arms fire. In the background another truck is visible. [Fortepan/Hajdú Fedő]

Soldier of 2nd Company of the 15th Bicycle Battalion crossed the River Dniester at Nizna on the wrecks of a destroyed bridge on 6 of July. The troops captured a bridgehead on the other side of the river. [Fortepan/Csorba]

Hungarian and German officers discussing the tactical situation at the destroyed bridge on the River Dniester on 6 July 1941, in the background a captured Soviet soldiers heading to the captivity. The Hungarian officers from left to right are 1st Lieutenant Géza Páldy commander of the 2nd Bicycle Company and 1st Lieutenant Miklós Holló, commander of the Sapper Platoon. [P. Mujzer]

Members of the 2nd Bicycle Company approached the pillar on wooden planks built by the sappers and climbing on the ladders with their bicycles on their shoulders, the backpacks, and kits attached to the 32M military bicycles left behind to ease the weight. [P. Mujzer]

Troopers of the 2nd Company of the 15th Bicycle Battalion climbing on a makeshift ladder into the top of the bridge pillar with his 32M military bicycles. At the bottom of the bridge pillar two reconnaissance troopers, armed but dressed in civilian clothes waiting their turn to cross the bridge on the same day. [Fortepan/Csorba]

The Soviet sappers just partially demolished the bridges, which made the repair easier for the Hungarian troops. This bridge was demolished at the River Dniester between Mihalecz and Ustecko. [Fortepan/Teller]

Hungarian engineer troops rebuilding the bridge between Mihalecz and Ustecko on the River Dniester in July 1941. The engineers used the existing bridge structure and the wreckages to built the new wooden temporary bridge. [Fortepan]

The advance of the Hungarian troops towards Kolomea placed the entire right flank of the Soviet 18th Army, under threat of attack. Evaluating the situation, General Smirnov, the commander of the army, ordered the commander of the 96th Mountain Rifle Division to withdraw units to the northern bank of the Seret River and take up a defense on the Berkhomet-Glybokaya sector.

The advancing Hungarian troops were able to take only a mere 10 kilometers in four days, even the motor vehicles were more of a hindrance than a help. The mountain captured the heavily defended town of Tatarovo, on the northeast foothills of the Carpathian Mountain on 02 July.

The first phase of the operation was dominated by the Hungarian mountain and border guard troops, which slowly opened up the passes and repaired the destroyed bridges. It enabled the Mobile Corps to cross the Carpathian Mountains and pursuit the withdrawing Soviet forces.

In these days in June-July 1941, the breakthrough by Axis units in the Yarmolyntsi region threatened the Kamenets-Podol'skiy Fortified Region and divisions of the Soviet 17th Rifle Corps, with a thrust from the north and rear. From the west, units of the Hungarian Mobile Corps advanced along the northern bank of the Dniester River, toward Kamenets-Podol'skiy.

The 18th and 12th Soviet Armies withdrew alongside the River Pruth. According to the Hungarian estimation, the Soviet troops performed an organized retreat, demolishing bridges, mining the roads and key positions.

After the initial difficulties, the Mobile Corps started its advance into the Stanislav plains, spearheaded by the 2nd Motorised Rifle Brigade. It took Deliatyn on 02 July; the town was captured by the troops of the 6th Motorised Rifle Battalion approaching on foot. The Battalion headed towards Kolomea, annihilated 150 men strong Soviet rearguard, and took the town. The local population celebrated the Hungarian troops with garlands. The friendly attitude was due to the brutal

The rest of the 15th Bicycle Battalion crossed the River Dniester on 7 July by ferries made of pontoons and bridge walkways to ferry bicycle squads with their weapons, bicycles manually operated by the sappers. [War Correspondent Company]

Troopers of the 15th Bicycle Battalion assemble for crossing at the riverbank of the Dniester. The troops waited for the ferries in the open space without any air defense precautions. The Hungarian soldiers carry their old-style WW1 backpack housing the spare ammunition and hand grenades. The rest of the kit is attached to their military bicycles. [War Correspondent Company]

Hungarian troops crossing the River Dniester on ferry pushed by four metal hull motorboat powered by outboard engines. The ferry transported two Ford-Marmon trucks and one Mercedes G5 staff car. [Fortepan/Csorba]

38M Botond all-terrain squad carrier trucks belonged to the 4th Hungarian Motorised Rifle Battalion crossing a makeshift bridge on the River Pruth. The white square unit sign visible on the back of the trucks. [War Correspondent Company]

Hungarian soldiers of the II. Engineer Battalion lined up at the new military bridge built between Mihalecz and Ustecko on the River Dniester in July 1941. The River Dniester had a characteristic steep river bank on the east side. [Fortepan/Teller]

massacre committed by the NKVD troops against the local population.

The Hungarian Mobile Corps occupied Kolomea, establishing communications with the right-flank units of the German 17th Army.

On 4 July the 2nd Mountain Battalion performed reconnaissance towards Vigoda, at River Styr contacted with the German troops, who first fired on the Hungarian mountain, one-one soldier wounded in each side.

The commander of the 2nd Motorised Rifle Brigade ordered the 5th Motorised Rifle Battalion and 2/4th Howitzer Battery to advance from Kolomea to Horodenka on 04 July. The 5th Motorised Rifle Battalion advanced quickly; the rear guard passed through Kolomea and approached Horodenka. At the village, the Hungarians came under the concentrated fire of the Soviet rear-guards, about two infantry battalions.

Sappers of the II. Hungarian Engineer Battalion at the demolished bridge over the River Dniester at Mihalec and Ustenko. The Hungarians built their own 33M military bridge next to the demolished Soviet one. [Fortepan/ Ungváry]

Hungarian WM-21 Hawk short-range reconnaissance/light bomber planes of the VIII and the X Short Range Reconnaissance Squadrons take off from a military airfield heading towards the Soviet targets. The flights of the two squadrons fly in V formation, following each other in. On the ground a Focke-Wulf FW 58 Weihe liaison plan, canvas hangars are visible. [Fortepan/ Varga dr.]

Ford-Marmon truck with ex-Polish fuel trailer belonged to the supply column of the 3rd Hungarian Motorised Rifle Battalion in July 1941 in the Carpathian Mountains. Stick bundles attached to the mudguard of the truck. [Fortepan/Hajdú Fedő]

Resting Ford-Marmon truck of the 3rd Hungarian Motorised Rifle Battalion in the valley of the Carpathian Mountain with local Polish civilians and horsed wagon. The civilian on the left dressed in Hungarian Army boots and trousers with officer belt looks a bit suspicious, probably belonged to a Hungarian undercover reconnaissance team. [Fortepan/Hajdú Fedő]

Hungarian cavalrymen of the 4th Hussar Regiment entering into Gwozdzie on 09 July 1941, the local population peacefully observing the Hungarian troops. [Illésfalvi]

Destroyed Railway Bridge over the River Bug. Just the pillars of the bridge were blown up by the Soviet engineers. The Hungarian troops reached the River Bug by the end of July 1941. [Fortepan/Berkó]

German supply column somewhere in Ukraine, the vehicles had a white circular shape unit sign. The staff car is a Mercedes; the soldiers belonged to a Flak unit wearing Luftwaffe uniforms. [Fortepan/Berkó]

Hungarian tankette platoon, equipped with 35M Fiat Ansaldo tankettes belonged to the 1st Armoured Cavalry Battalion parking alongside the fence of a destroyed official building probably in Tulchin, Ukraine, summer of 1941. [Fortepan/Berkó]

The Hungarian motorized rifles broke into the village of Horodenka and in close combat captured and cleaned it, house after house.

On 04 July the 15th Bicycle Battalion, commanded by Lieutenant Colonel Erik Bresztovszky reached the 200-meter long wood bridge at River Lomnica. It was partially demolished by the Soviet sappers but was still passable for infantry. The bicycle troops crossed the river and secured the bridgehead. Meanwhile, the rest of the battalion started to wad the river with motor vehicles. One Hansa Lloyd half-tracked artillery tractor was pulled over the chest-deep river with ropes and manpower. Two 38M Botond trucks were also pushed across the River. The troops and officers worked together, some of them were in the river the others help to operate the winches to pull over the vehicles and guns. The battalion commander sent ahead reconnaissance patrols to Stanislav, they reported the town empty of Soviet troops. The troops of the 15th Bicycle Battalion advanced 180 kilometers within 36 hours on difficult mountainous terrain. Most of the time pushing their military bicycles, climbing and descending on mountain roads through passes varied from 750 to 1229 meters high.

The 12th Bicycle Battalion's patrols belonged to the 2nd Motorised Rifle Brigade also reached the city at the same time. Significant war booty was captured at Stanislav, among them were two I-16 fighter planes, 6 heavy, 8 medium, and 18 light tanks, 25 tracked artillery tractors, 50 trucks, and 5 cars. The Hungarians also seized military stores with food, ammunition, tires, and fuel dumps with 10000 litter fuels. These catches were vital for the Hungarians to keep going.

Major General János Vörös, commander of the 2nd Motorised Rifle Brigade organized a battle group on 5 July; from the 4th, 5th Motorised Rifle and the 12th Bicycle Battalions commanded by Colonel Antal Benda. Its task was to capture the bridge over the River Dniester at Zaleshchiki, intact.

The 6th Motorised Rifle Battalion captured Kitzman, a major road intersection on the morning of 5 July. The

Town of Tulchin at the time when Hungarian troops entering into the town, at the Veterinary School. An abandoned Soviet T-26 light tank was left behind. [Fortepan/Berkó]

Graves of fallen German SS soldiers photographed by the Hungarians, killed in action on 06 July 1941 at Husiatin, Ukraine. Gefreiter Sepp Schmidt belonged to the 15th Westland Regiment. [Fortepan/Csorba]

Soldiers of the 15th Bicycle Battalion posing to the camera during their lunch break, cooking pancakes on a campfire, armed with an 8mm 31M light machine gun. [Fortepan/Csorba]

3rd Company was in the town when its reconnaissance patrol reported enemy trucks coming from Chernovtsy. The 50 Soviet troops belonged to the Soviet 28th Cavalry Division. The Hungarian company commander deployed his motorized rifles outside of the town at the road intersection. Soon the Hungarians found themselves under attack by a Soviet battalion-size force. The battalion commander Lieutenant Colonel Keményfy ordered his battalion to repel the attacking Soviet forces. The Soviet advance collapsed and the Red Army troops started to withdraw. But soon the Soviet units counter-attacked the Hungarian motorized rifles. The battalion commander reported his status to the Brigade. He was instructed to keep his position, wait for the reinforcement, which consisted of an armored car platoon and one motorized rifle company from the 4th Motorised rifle Battalion. The Hungarian Air Force also supported the land forces; the Heinkel He 46 type reconnaissance planes of the

VII Short-range Reconnaissance Squadron strafed and bombed the Soviet forces with10 kilogram anti-personal bombs. Finally, the 6th Motorised Rifle Battalion was able to hold his position and keep it until the night when the Soviet troops withdrew from the area.

The battalion lost 12 men killed in action.

The clashes with the Soviet troops highlighted the superior firepower of the Red Army in contrast with the Hungarian weaponry. The Soviet troops were well equipped with submachine guns; self-loading rifles the Hungarians had none of these. The Hungarian motorized rifle battalions only had one mortar platoon with two medium mortars.

The River Dniester reached by the Hungarian on 5 July between the towns of Zaleshchiki and Michalcze.

The 15th Bicycle battalion reaches the River Dniester on that day at Nizna and found both bridges; the road and railway bridge demolished. However, the road bridge was just partially destroyed. The bridge structure collapsed into the flooded river between the bridge getaway and the first pillar. The commander of the 2nd Bicycle Company, 1st Lieutenant Géza Páldy, and 1st Lieutenant Miklós Holló, commander of the Sapper Platoon ordered the troops to check the bridge and prepare a temporal construction for crossing. The Hungarian sappers and bicycle troopers collected wood planks and built a tread to the first pillar. Then a 10-meter high ladder was constructed and attached to the pillar. The Hungarians

Soldiers of the 15th Bicycle Battalion posing with their 32M military bicycle produced by the Weiss Manfred Factory, a heavy but durable piece. Holding the bicycle on hand required certain physical strength. [Fortepan/Csorba]

Abandoned Soviet T-26 tank, most likely left behind due to mechanical failure or lack of fuel. Behind the Soviet tank is a Ford-Marmon truck that belonged to the 3rd Hungarian Motorised Rifle Battalion, packed with fuel drums. [Fortepan/Hajdú Fedő]

Soviet T-28 heavy tank blown up by its crew, the tank probably had an engine failure, the engine deck opened. The internal explosion throws into the air its turret. [Fortepan/Csorba]

Soldiers of the 15th Bicycle Battalion posing on an abandoned Soviet T-26 light tank, on the left is a staff sergeant, on the right the soldier dressed in mechanic overall with leather photo camera case. [Fortepan/Csorba]

climbed on the ladder to the top of the bridge pillar, after that the bridge was intact to proceed. First, a foot patrol was sent to take a covering position on the other side of the river. The bicycle troopers climbed on the ladder carry their military bicycles on their shoulders. It was a splendid achievement carrying their 32M Weis Manfred military bicycle, a sturdy but heavy piece. The 2nd Company deployed civilian clothed reconnaissance

Hungarian 37mm 36M anti-tank gun in a blocking position on the edge of the village of Kirmasowka on 24 July 1941. The anti-tank gun belonged to the advance guard of the 4th Motorised Rifle Battalion which came under heavy Soviet artillery barrage. In the background a burned-out 38M Botond truck and a stable. [NL-HANA]

Camouflaged Hungarian 35M Fiat Ansaldo tankette with Hungarian made observation cupola parking next to a village football field somewhere in Ukraine. The platoon and company commander's vehicles had observation cupolas. [Fortepan/Ludovika]

teams, Hungarian enlisted men with local language knowledge (Ukrainian), and local guides to explore the area of advance. It was not allowed by the rule of war, but a useful device to detect the enemy.

The sappers found a damaged ferry on the river bank and started to repair it. However, by the evening of that day, just the bicycle platoons could cross the river.

The 2nd Bicycle Company started its advance on 7 July towards Liszovce, took 30 kilometers, and surprised the Soviet forces preparing for demolition of the bridge over River Siret. The company led by 1st Lieutenant Géza Páldy captured and secure the bridge intact and taken 10 prisoners of war.

5 July 1941, in the military diary of General Franz Halder, continued to complain about the poor condition of the roads in the zone of Army Group South.

The withdrawing 6th, 26th, and 12th Soviet Armies were constantly threatened with envelopment by the 1st German Panzer Group and by the 17th Army from the north and later the 11th Army from the south.

The resistance of troops of the Southwest Front was stubborn. At the same time, on the front of the German

Abandoned Soviet T-26 light tank with special camouflage paint and doted white stripe painted on the turret. [Fortepan/Hajdú Fedő]

Hungarian officers posing on a captured Soviet fort, second from right is Lieutenant Colonel Zoltán Pisky founder and organizer of the Hungarian mountain troops, commander of the 2nd Mountain Battalion during the operation in 1941. [Fortepan/Mészöly]

17th Army and Hungarian troops, disorderly withdrawal of the Soviet units was taking place. In some places, an accumulation of several columns on one highway was seen, with crowds of refugees wedging themselves into the columns of infantry.

The II and VIII Bicycle Battalions established a bridgehead on the Soviet-held side of River Dniester at Nizna on 06 July. On 07 July the town of Tultse was captured with a halfway intact bridge on the River. It was fortunate luck for the advancing Hungarian troops; the

38M Botond truck belonged to the 2nd Motorised Rifle Battalion wade through a creek. The driver and the co-driver wearing the 37M Italian-style crash helmets. The unit sign, white oblique stripe painted on the right mudguard. [War Correspondent Company]

Units of the 4th Hussar Regiment marching under a welcoming arch erected by the local Ukrainian population to cross an intact wooden bridge over the River Dniester. [Illésfalvi]

motorized elements of the 2nd Motorised Rifle Brigade arrived just in time to achieve a surprise crossing over the repaired bridge at Zaleshchiki on 07 July. The next day the 1st Motorised Rifle and the 1st Cavalry Brigades also crossed the river.

The 1st Motorised Rifle Brigades deployed just on 30 June from its peacetime garrisons around Budapest after completing its mobilization. Crossing through the Tatarov Pass advanced on the nonexisting road towards Kolomea. The 1st Motorised Brigade was not involved in actual fighting in this stage of the operation. It provided cover for the southern flank of the advancing 2nd Motorised Rifle Brigade.

The hussar regiments and the horsed elements of the 1st Cavalry Brigade disembarked at Körösmező-Tiszaborkút on 02 July to meet their motorized and bicycle units, which were already there in the assembly area.

The 1st Motorised Rifle Brigade crossed the River Zbruch at Skala on 09 July, which was the old Polish border into the Soviet Union.

As the troops of the Carpathian Operational Group reached into the plain terrain, mobility becomes a key issue for the advancing Hungarian units. In the less mobile part of the Carpathian Group, the troops of the VIII Corps were assigned to clearing up the already occupied rear areas and secure the lines of communications, to perform the standard occupational, security duties.

The crossing of the Carpathian Mountains and the muddy roads exhausted the troops' horses and motor vehicles as well. Instead of rest and maintenance, the Hungarian Mobile Corps was assigned to the Panzer Group 1 by the Army Group South.

From 9 July, the Mobile Corps was subordinated to the German Army Group South, to support the 17th German Army. The Mobile Corps had 1717 officers, 41790 men, 7529 horses, 1037 horse carriages, and 4372 motor vehicles.

From the beginning of the hostilities until 9 July, the Carpathian Operational Group lost 136 men killed, 344 wounded and 91 missing in action.

The second phase of the Hungarian operation covered the period of 9 July to 10 August and focused on the push to the River Bug.

Operation of the Mobile Corps

From July 9, the Mobile Corps was subordinated to the German Army Group South, to support the 17th German Army, while the VIII Corps remained in the rear areas to act as a security force.

The second phase of the Hungarian operation covered the period of 9 July to 10 August and focused on the push to the River Bug.

The Soviet commander General Kirponos ordered his 6th Army reinforced with the 16th and 15th Mechanised Corpses to hold firmly south of Berdichev, to protect the left-wing of the Southwest Front.

The Hungarian air reconnaissance sorties proved that the troops of the Soviet 17th Rifle corps, 18th Army retreating ahead of the Mobile Corps. The weather played on the Soviets side, the pouring rain transformed the roads into impassable terrain.

The troops of the 2nd Motorised rifle Brigade conquer Kamenets-Podol'skiy on 10 July. The 1st Motorised rifle Brigade advanced towards Smotryez-Landskorna-Balin.

On 11 July 1941, the Soviet 18th Mechanized Corps (39th, 47th Tank Divisions, 218th Motorized Division) received a mission to concentrate behind the right flank of the South Front in the region of Krasnovo. Toward the end of 11 July, units of the 47th Tank Division and 218th Motorized Division concentrated in the region of Zholoby, Komar Gorod, and Tomashpol, having on strength 249 tanks. The 39th Tank Division originally belonged to the 16th Mechanised Corps (208 tanks) was on the march, following the deployment area of the Corps, and by 15 July arrived in the region of Gorishkovka, Vapnyarka.

Due to the transfer of several rifle divisions and the 16th Mechanized Corps for operations on a different strategic axis, 20 divisions remained on strength with the Southern Front, with which to oppose the enemy, whose strength had increased on account of the Hungarian Mobile Corps entering operations. The Hungarian Corps was leading the advance to Mogilev-Podolsk along the northern bank of the Dniestr River. In total, the German 11th Army, the 3rd and 4th Romanian Armies, and the Hungarian Mobile Corps numbered 24 divisions, of which 16 divisions and 10 brigades, concentrated into three strike groups, were

The road between Tulchin and Kamenec-Podolsk knocked out the Soviet T-26 light tank and destroyed trucks in July 1941. [Fortepan/Berkó]

Knocked out Soviet T-26 light tank on the road between Tulchin and Kamanec-Podolsk. The Soviet tank was hit by several times by different caliber anti-tank weapons, most likely 50, 37, and 20mm rounds. [Fortepan/Berkó]

Hungarian motorized rifle squad in light combat order embarking on the makeshift ferry to cross the river. These kinds of river crossings were risky operations bearing in mind that the majority of the troopers simply could not swim. [NL-HaNa]

Next to the military bridge the bicycle troops crossing the River Bug on a makeshift bridge built of wooden planks, strong enough to take the weight of the bicycle troopers. On the 33M bridge Krupp Protze trucks crossing the river, in the background motorcycles and a Hansa Lloyd artillery tractor visible. [War Correspondent Company]

advancing in the first echelon. At the end of July 3 Italian division joined the Axis forces too. The numerical superiority in tanks and aviation remained on the side of the Southern Front, but it was unsuccessful in actualizing this.

The motorized rifle battalions of the 2nd Motorised Rifle Brigade earned a well-deserved rest and maintenance period after they captured Kamenets-Podol'skiy, on 9 July. Finally, the mobilized reservists of the battalions could join their units two weeks after the outbreak of the hostilities. The three motorized rifle battalions finally reached their operational strength.

The Mobile Corps commander requested the cavalry to advance and replace the motorized troops, which were stuck in the deep mud on 11 July. From 10 to 12

Brigade artillery, 105mm 37M light howitzer towed by 37M Hansa Lloyd half-tracked artillery tractor, crossing the River Bug on 33M military bridge laid on pontoons. [War Correspondent Company]

Motorized rifles crossing the River Bug with their 38M Botond truck followed by a dispatch rider on a Puch motorcycle on the 33M military bridge lay on pontoons. [NL-HANA]

of July, the Mobile Corps captured 13 enemy tanks, 12 guns, and 11 trucks.

The cavalry patrols of the 4th Hussar Regiment ambushed a withdrawing Soviet motorized column in a narrow valley at Tarasovka. The panicked Soviet soldiers left behind 100-150 trucks, artillery pieces and four-barrel anti-aircraft machine guns mounted on trucks.

Baptism of fire of the Armoured Troops

On the afternoon of 12 July, two platoons of the 3rd and one platoon from the 4th Light Tank Companies under the leadership of Captain Tibor Kárpáthy were subordinated to the battle group of Colonel Carl Püchler,

Armoured Car Company of the 2nd Armoured Cavalry Battalion was temporarily subordinated to the Carpathian Operational Group; the 39M Csaba armored cars washed in a small river at the Eastern slope of the Carpathian Mountains. [War Correspondent Company]

Advancing troops of the Mobile Corps, the cavalry squadrons, and the horsed supply wagons moving next to the road. The trucks and the light tank company of the 11th Light Tank Battalion moving on the highway, the license plate, H-324 indicate that the 38M Toldi tank belonged to the 11th Light Tank Battalion. [War Correspondent Company]

Enlisted NCOs of the 15th Bicycle Battalion dressed in light weighted summer uniform, bivouacking in the woods. Behind them, their double tent made of the camouflaged half-ponchos of the men. [Fortepan/Csorba]

Supply column of the 15th Bicycle Battalion waiting on a dirt road in the woods. The last vehicle is a Krupp Protze towing an ex-Polish fuel trailer; the next is a Ford truck. [Fortepan/Csorba]

commander of the 228th Jager Regiment, German 101st Jager/ Light Infantry Division.

About 13.00 hours of 13 July, Captain Tibor Kárpáthy was tasked to advance through Minkovtsy and Antonowka and capture the Height 306 south of the village Filjanowka. The advancing forces consisted of three platoons of Hungarian 38M Toldi light tanks, one German bicycle company(101st Bicycle Battalion), two German anti-tank platoons, and a German artillery battalion providing fire support. Based on the German reconnaissance just 5-6 enemy machine-gun posts and covering infantry was in position north of the road.

The Hungarian 38M Toldi light tanks crossed a creek at Minkovtsy at 16.30 hours and reached Antonowka at 17.00 hours. Captain Kárpáthy deployed his two 37mm, anti-tank gun platoons, alongside the road and the tank platoons flanking the village on both sides. The Soviet troops surrounded, and the Hungarian German troops captured 200 Soviet prisoners of war with heavy weapons.

The Hungarian light tank company advanced to capture Novaya Ushitsa. The leading platoon commanded by 2nd Lieutenant Alfonz Dorsan approaching on the road was followed by the company's Staff with Captain Kárpáthy and the rest of the two light tank platoons.

On the left side of the road about company strength Soviet infantry armed with machine guns, hiding in the agricultural field.

The Company Staff and the 3/II Platoon commanded by Candidate Sergeant Péter Hábel deployed to attack. The I Platoon, overcome the Height 306 north of the road capturing a third Soviet anti-tank gun. So far just one 38M Toldi light tank was damaged with no casualties. Captain Kárpáthy and his Staff's light tanks also reached the Height 306. The Company Commander sent back reporting one of his light tanks to Colonel Püchler.

At 17.30 hours the advance continued, 2nd Lieutenant Dorsan leading platoon reached the edge of the village of Filjanowka at twilight. The Lieutenant and

Fallen Hungarian soldier belonged to the 3rd Motorised Rifle Battalion laying on the stretcher, the death certificate and his dog tag attached to his field jacket. [Fortepan/Hajdú Fedő]

Soldiers of the 15th Bicycle Battalion condolence their fallen German comrades hastily buried in the local village cemetery in the summer of 1941. [Fortepan/Csorba]

Hungarian soldiers at the fortification of the Stalin line posing with a captured Soviet Maxim machine gun. The fortifications were abandoned by the Red Army without significant resistance. [Fortepan/Hajdú Fedő]

Another view of the Soviet bunker with impacts of the small arms fire around the portholes and the Soviet 7,62mm Maxim machine gun on wheeled Sokolov mounting. [Fortepan/Hajdú Fedő]

his crew did not discover a camouflaged Soviet 45mm anti-tank gun, which knocked out both Hungarian tanks. 2nd Lieutenant Dorsan was wounded on his leg, his two crew members were killed in action. He had no radio communication, could not notice the danger to his comrades.

Captain Kárptáhy and his platoon commander went forward to clear the situation. The Soviet anti-tank gun from a distance of 200-300meters knocked out the company commander's Toldi tank. The driver and the gunner were killed instantly, Captain Kárpáthy seriously injured, could not leave his tank. The commander's Toldi

The damaged main building of Rail Way Station at Tovsztve and a crashed Soviet SB-2 bomber planes. [Fortepan/Kiss]

The battered main building of the Rail Way Station of Tovszte, the building inherited from the Habsburg Monarchy, same stations can be found in Hungary, Slovakia, Poland, and Austria as well. [Fortepan/Csorba]

Railway Station of Tovszte, Ukraine, heavily damaged by the air raids. Destroyed rolling stocks inspected by Hungarian soldiers. [Fortepan/Csorba]

lay helpless waiting for the next shot. At that moment his platoon commander Candidate-Sergeant Pál Habel rushed in and halted between the enemy and the damaged Toldi, protecting his company commander. The next shot hit this brave Toldi light tank and all of its crew perished. The rest of the company deployed to combat, outflanked the village. During the clashes, further two 38M Toldi light tank was destroyed. The German troops just reached the Hungarian positions at 19.50 hours. 2nd Lieutenant Imre Kömlődy took over the command from Captain Kárpáthy, who was evacuated from the battlefield.

During the baptize of fire of the 3rd Light Tank Company suffered 60% causalities, six 38M Toldi have knocked out the number plates of the destroyed 38. M Toldis were: H-306,-314,-315,-316,-397,-399. Nine crewmen were killed. Out of the nine crew, 8 were killed due to the impact of the Soviet armored piercing shells. However, due to the thin armor of the 38M Toldi light tanks, the Soviet armored-piercing shells did not blow inside the vehicles just went through the tanks killing, injuring the crew. On the other hand, these knocked-out tanks were repairable.

The Soviet troops suffered 40-50 men killed in action, 8-10 machine guns, 5 anti-tank guns captured one tank knocked out. According to a report from HQ Soviet Southern Front; *on 14 July, at Novaya Ushitsa 13 enemy tanks were destroyed and Hungarian documents were found on the dead crew.*

The Soviet antitank weapons were superior to every Hungarian armored vehicle. Even the anti-tank rifles could penetrate the lightly armored Hungarian 38M Toldi tanks and 39M Csaba armored cars. The Ansaldo tankettes were vulnerable to infantry fire too. The Soviet

German motorized medium artillery advancing on a dusty road, the German Sdk. Fz. 8 half-tracked artillery tractor towing the 150mm howitzer. [Fortepan/Berkó]

German supply truck column moving on the dusty road towards the River Dnieper, the leading vehicle is an Opel Blitz truck. [Fortepan/Berkó]

German supply column lead by a staff car and dispatch riders belonged to the Kleist Operational Group. The large white K stands for the Kleist Group painted on the mudguard. [Fortepan/Berkó]

45mm armored-piercing shells simply went through the chassis of the Hungarian armored vehicles without detonating.

The commander of the 1st Motorized Rifle Brigade, Major General Jenő Major protested at the commander of 101st Germans Light Division, Lieutenant General Brauner von Haydringen because the Hungarian light tanks were used for breaking through the enemy lines, which were out of their possibilities.

On 15 July the German LII Corps troops, the 100th and 101st Light/Jager Divisions broken into the fortification of the Stalin Line. The fortified line was defended by the mixed units of the 44th, 58th, 164th, and 72nd Rifle Divisions.

German anti-aircraft artillery unit armed with 20mm Flak canon at Pervomajsk on the riverside of the Bug, in the background the building of the power station visible. [Fortepan/Berkó]

Pilots of the 2/3 Fighter Squadron in readiness waiting for the mission at the airfield of Kolomya mid-July 1941. On the right side of the picture is Captain Aladár Szobránczy (Negró), the squadron commander. The Captain's Danish Dog, called Ricsi was the mascot of the fighter squadron. Its picture as a shoulder patch was worn by the crew on their overalls. [War Correspondent Company]

From 15 to 17of July, the VI and VIII Bicycle Battalions were given a short rest at Kamenets-Podol'skiy. The bicycle troops were exhausted due to the rapid rate of advance over bad roads. The bicycles were severely damaged, tires are worn out.

The divisions of the Soviet 17th Rifle Corps were conducting battles on a wide front southwest of Zhmerinka, against units of the German 17th Army; the Hungarian Mobile Corps in the region of Kopai-Gorod; and against units of the Romanian 3rd Army, 25 kilometers northwest of Mogilev-Podolski on 17 July 1941.

Due to the large number of mechanical problems occurring among the armored and motor vehicles; civilian technician groups were organized and sent to the front from the Manfred Weiss, Ganz, and MAVAG Factories on July 18. A separate group was organized to deal with the 30 mechanically broken-down Ansaldo tankettes.

The 1st Motorised Rifle and the 1st Cavalry Brigades were requested by the commander of the German 17th Army to join the breakthrough the Stalin Line. The terrain was very difficult, with swamps, crossed by rivers. The 1st Motorised Rifle Brigade launched its attack from Dunajec and broke through the fortified line at Bar on July 19.

The commander of the 1st Cavalry Brigade organized his troops into two groups. The motorized and cyclist elements attacked on the road and the mounted units were deployed over the rough terrain. The Hussars launched a successful surprise attack on July 20.

The Soviet 47th Tank Division attacked the German 100th Light Division on 19-20 July, which was on the

Flight Sergeant Árpád Kertész welcomed by the squadron mascot, Ricsi upon his arrival back from his sortie. He shot down a Soviet reconnaissance plane at Stanislaw on 27 June 1941. Behind the pilot is his Fiat Cr.42 biplane. [War Correspondent Company]

right flank of the German 17th Army. The 1st Motorised Rifle Brigade was tasked to support the Germans. The 9th Light Tank Battalion, the 1st Motorised Rifle Battalion, and the 1/4th Howitzer Battery were alarmed and sent to relieve the German troops. Temporarily the 1st Motorised Rifle Brigade was subordinated to the German LII. Corps.

On 21 July the troops of the 1st Motorised Brigade assembled for the attack toward Rogosna, their goal was to reach the River Bug. The first wave of the attacking Hungarian troops consisted of the 3rd Motorised Rifle Battalion in the center, on its right the 1st Motorised Rifle, on the left the 9th Tank Battalions, the 1st Mechanised Artillery Battalion provided fire support to the troops, the 1st Reconnaissance and 2nd Motorised Rifle Battalions kept in reserve. The 10th and VIII Bicycle Battalions remained behind as the second echelon.

The victory marks are painted on the tail of Staff Sergeant Sándor Szobránci's (Szoják) Fiat Cr.42 biplane. The pilot already shot down two Slovakian planes in 1939. The victory marks are painted with a template; however, the military insignia was hand-painted. [War Correspondent Company]

WM-21 Hawk short-range reconnaissance planes flying over a Hungarian 36M 40mm Bofors autocannon position, returning from a sortie in Ukraine, summer of 1941. [War Correspondent Company]

Hungarian Caproni Ca.135 bomber plane prepared for the mission, the ground crew loading the 250-kilogram bombs into the bomb bay of the aircraft. This plane belonged to the 3rd Bomber Group, 3/5 "Witch" Bomber Squadron, its sister squadron deployed to Ukraine in 1941. [War Correspondent Company]

The attack developed on difficult terrain, the heavy weapons lagged behind the attacking troops. The 1st Motorised Rifle Battalion bumped into enemy resistance, the 1/1st Howitzer Battery knocked out three Soviet tanks with direct fire in support of the motorized rifles. The advance guard of the 3rd Motorised Rifle Battalion wanted to liberate an encircled German unit when was surrounded by Soviet forces at Rogosna in battalion-size supported with tanks. The Hungarian battalion commander ordered his reserve to open the encirclement and at the same time, he led his troop to break out. The German and Hungarian anti-tank guns knocked out 15

Soviet tanks. Finally, the 3rd Motorised Rifle Battalion could capture the village of Rogosna by the evening. The Soviet 47Th Tank Division lost 93 tanks due to the German, Hungarian anti-tank guns' fire.

The 1st Motorised Rifle Brigade knocked out 21 Russian tanks, 16 armored cars, and 12 guns from 19 to 22 July. The Hungarian casualties amounted to 26 killed, 50 wounded, and 10 missing soldiers, with 15 armored vehicles damaged. Seven 38M Toldi out of a dozen were repairable, but the three Csaba armored cars were beyond the field repair.

Battle around Gordievka

On 23 July the Mobile Corps's units reached the River Bug and accomplished its first operational objective. The German 17th Army, after crossing the River Bug headed towards Uman to encircle the 6th and 12th Soviet Armies – under the command of Lieutenant General I. N. Muzychenko and Major General P. G. Ponedelin.

On July 23 the 5th Motorised Rifle Battalion clashed with strong Russian forces. The 1st Horsed Artillery Battalion supported the riflemen with their aging 80mm field guns, destroying the enemy with directly aimed fire. The 1st Cavalry Brigade covered 585 kilometers during 8 marching and 9 battle days.

In connection with the battle of Uman, the troops of the Hungarian Mobile Corps turned to the southwest direction to destroy the Soviet forces embedded at the Bug River bend. In the lead with the 2nd Motorised Rifle Brigade attacked in the direction of Tulchin on 23 July. The Armoured Car Company of the 2nd Reconnaissance Battalion supported the German 257th Infantry Division to capture Tulchin. The 1st Cavalry Brigade followed the motorized rifles as a reserve.

The Soviet Army secured the River crossing for their troops over the Bug. To support it, strong battle groups with artillery were positioned on the right side of the River Bug against the advancing Hungarian units.

From 24 July, the 2nd Motorised rifle Brigade's battalions attacked towards the Railway Station of Demkowka and the railway line. The 11th Tank, 5th, and 6th Motorised Rifle Battalions engaged with superior Soviet forces. The defending Soviet troops were reinforced and a regimental size unit of the Soviet 209th Mountain Rifle Regiment / 96th Mountain Division launched a series of counter-attacks against the Hungarians from Danidovka. The Soviet counter-strikes were lead and coordinated by Colonel Ivan Mihajlovic Shepetov, the commander of the soviet 96th Mountain Rifle Division.

The units of the 2nd Motorised Rifle Brigade were unable to clear the situation. Finally, the troops of the 2nd Reconnaissance, 12th Bicycle, and the 4th, 5th, 6th

Field maintenance of the Fiat Cr.42 fighter biplane belonged to the 2/3 Fighter Squadron with the unit sign dog head painted on the fuselage. The two white bars painted on the tail section represent two air victories. [Fortepan/ Kerekes]

Abandoned Soviet Ba-20 light armored car with Hungarian, German soldiers and a local boy inside the vehicle. A surprisingly intact bridge is visible in the background. [Fortepan/Csorba]

Motorised rifle Battalions reached the line of Kirnasovka- South – Bogdanovka, losing 2 dead, 23 wounded, and on missing soldiers.

The right flank of the Brigade was covered by the 3rd Cavalry Regiment of the 8th Romanian Cavalry Brigade, which withdrew after the first contact with the Soviet Forces, which left undefended the Hungarian flank.

The Germans were aware of the hostile relationship between the Hungarians and Romanians. The German Army strictly regulated the borderline between

Abandoned Soviet Ba-10 armored car resting on the side of the road. Its main armament, the 45mm anti-tank gun was formidable against the lightly armored Hungarian tanks. Next to the armored car the drum magazines of the machine guns scattered on the ground. [Fortepan/Csorba]

Abandoned Soviet Ba-10 armored car surrounded by Hungarian soldiers. In front of the armored car are visible the tracks which could attach to the rear wheels to improve the cross country capability of the armored car. [Fortepan/Hajdú Fedő]

Camouflaged Krupp Protze half squad carrier truck belonged to the Heavy Weapon Company of the 4th Motorised Rifle Battalion, armed with 8mm 07/31M Schwarzlose machine gun on an anti-aircraft tripod. The battalion's unit sign was painted on the mudguard of the truck. [P. Mujzer]

the advancing Hungarian and Romanian forces, it was forbidden to cross each other are of operation, which was not always easy during a mobile operation. According to the Hungarian reports, the Romanian troops advancing on parallel lines with the Hungarians always reported incorrectly their position to the Hungarians. In reality, the Romania troops were 20-30 kilometers back as it was reported. It always gave the

Abandoned Soviet Ba-10 armored cars and a Hungarian dispatch rider on DKW motorcycle. The tires of the Soviet armored car already removed by the Hungarians to replace their damaged ones. [Fortepan/Mészöly]

Advancing Krupp Protze belonged to the bicycle troops of the 9th Bicycle –Light Tank Battalion. The unit sign, white hand holding a double-cross, painted on the back of the truck. The 07/31M Schwarzlose machine gun ready to deploy on land mounting. [P. Mujzer]

Horse inspection of the Hussars in Ukraine summer of 1941. The long-distance marches and the defaults of 35M saddles worn down the horses of the cavalry. By August of 1941, half of the cavalry squadrons fought on foot. [Fortepan/Csorba]

Krupp Protze light anti-tank tractors park in front of a burned house, between the houses motor bicycles hidden from the aerial observation of the Red Air Force. The soldiers dressed in a great coat, mechanic overalls, and field tunic. [P. Mujzer]

Hungarian soldiers of the 15th Bicycle Battalion posing with the wreckage of a shot down Soviet SB 2 bomber plane. [Fortepan/Csorba]

One platoon of the 15th Bicycle Battalion posing on the shot down Soviet BS-2 bomber plane accompanied by a village boy. [Fortepan/Csorba]

possibility for the Soviet troops to flank the advancing Hungarian forces.

The 2nd Motorised Rifle Brigade found itself in danger. The brigade commander, Major General János Vörös re-deployed his tank battalion on the right flank of the Brigade, to replace the missing Romanians.

The Major General Miklós Dálnoki, commander of the Mobile Corps ordered the 1st Motorised Brigade, the 11th Bicycle-Tank, and the 1st Armoured Cavalry Battalions to turn back and support the units of the 2nd Brigade. The 1st Motorised Brigade reached the area only with great difficulties, because of the rainy weather and mud.

To support the motorized rifles, the Révhegyi Combat Group, consisted of the 1st Armoured Cavalry battalion, two bicycle companies, and 3rd Motorised Artillery Battalion was subordinated to the 2nd Motorised Rifle Brigade, lead by Colonel Ferenc Révhegyi, commander of the 1st Armoured Cavalry Battalion.

In the second half of 25 July, units of the German 17th Army and the Hungarian Mobile Corps penetrated the defenses of the 18th Soviet Mechanized Corps and the 17th Soviet Rifle Corps and conquered the regions of Gaisin, Ladyzhin, and Gubnik. At that time, the troops of the 18th Soviet Army were conducting ferocious battles on the Gaisin axis, against the advancing divisions of the German 17th Army and the Hungarian Mobile Corps, which we're striving to breakthrough in the general direction of Uman. Sub-units of the 18th Mechanized Corps abandoned Teplik and began a withdrawal in the southeast direction. Forward units of the Axis troops arrived in the region of Ternovka, 50km southeast of Gaisin.

Thc brigade commander of the 2nd Motorised Rifle Brigade dispatched his advance guard on 26 July from Letkivka towards Trosztyanec, whet it was fired upon from the nearby. The 4th Motorised Rifle Battalion advanced in the second wave was attacked too. The commander decided to annihilate the Soviet forces sending his advance guard; the 1st Armoured Cavalry, 13th and 14th Bicycle, 4th Motorised Rifle Battalions plus

The same Soviet SB-2 bomber plane was photographed from another angle without soldiers. The crash-landed bomber caught fire and except the rear fuselage burned out. [Fortepan/Csorba]

38M Toldi light tank passes through a Ukrainian village, the light tank still bearing the old unit sign of the white tank silhouette of the 2nd Reconnaissance Battalion, but already relocated to the 9th Light Tank Battalion. [Fortepan/Berkó]

38M Toldi light tanks of 9th Light Tank Battalion advancing in a small Ukrainian village, in the roadside an abandoned Soviet ST Stalinec tractor visible. [Fortepan/Berkó]

one-one light tank company and an artillery battery to frontal attack. While the 5th and 6th Motorised Rifle Battalions would flank the Soviet mountain troops from North through Gordievka. The 6th Motorised Rifle Battalion was able to capture the village of Gordievka and annihilate the defending Soviet battalion. The 3rd Motorised Rifle Company supported by the Machine Gun Company and the battalion mortar platoon broken into the village. The 1st Motorised Rifle Company attacked from the north and the 2nd Company was in reserve. During the fighting Soviet soldiers were taken prisoners in civilian cloth, executed on the spot according to the standard regulations. The stubbornly resisting Soviet troops embedded into the houses, refusing surrender. The Hungarians had no choice than using their 36M flame grenade to burn down the resisting positions. By the end of the day, the Hungarians move out of Gordievka to take a better defendable position outside of the village. The reconnaissance patrols interrogated Soviet prisoners confirmed assembling Soviet troops preparing an attack on next day.

The 2nd motorized Rifle Brigade suffered 25 men killed, 152 wounded men, in return captured 170 Soviet prisoners, 2 anti-tank guns, 5 mortars.

The 1st Motorised Rifle Brigade got the marching order on the early morning of 26 July to deploy and replace

Hungarian soldiers posing with an abandoned Soviet 152mm gun-howitzer, on the left is an ex-Polish Polski FIAT signal track. [Fortepan/Merza]

Abandoned Soviet T-60 light tank with Hungarian belonged to a supply column operating mobilized civilian trucks. The white title MATEOSZ stands for Hungarian Freight Carrier Association. [Fortepan/Merza]

the 2nd Motorised Rifle Brigade by 28 July. However, the heavy rain turned the nonexisting roads into mud pits, the destroyed bridges also slow down the redeployment.

The 1st Motorised Rifle Brigade should attack through Obodivka towards Bersad. The three motorized rifle battalions advanced in the first echelon, the reconnaissance and light tank battalions were the reserves.

On 27 July the 2nd Motorised Brigade's units also prepared to advance and clear the western bank of the River Bug from the stubbornly resisting Soviet forces. Colonel Révhegyi had its 1st Armoured Cavalry and the 12th, 13th, 14th Bicycle, 3rd Artillery Battalions to attack towards Demidivka, Bersad, Balanivka.

The Ankay Group, led by Colonel Győző Ankay-Anesini deputy commander of the 2nd Motorised rifle

Repairing the flat tire of the mobilized civilian Wanderer car, the headlights of the car covered with captured Soviet gas masks to provide blackout. The mobilized civilian trucks and cars technically were unreliable and broken down frequently. [Fortepan/Berkó]

Ford-Marmon truck of the supply column of the 3rd Motorised Rifle Battalion during a shortstop. The truck transported fuel drums and jerry cans to carry the daily fuel supply of the battalion. [Fortepan/Hajdú Fedő]

Due to the difficult terrain, the ex-Polish fuel trailer towing system disintegrated, on the left side of the photo a Ford-Marmon truck visible with the white vertical bar unit sign of the 3rd Motorised Rifle Battalion, the white T means Staff in Hungarian. [Fortepan/Hajdú Fedő]

Brigade, consisted of the motorized rifle battalions, the 11th Tank, 2nd Reconnaissance Battalions supported by two artillery battalions, and one 40mm Bofors battery should advance towards Bershad.

The attacking Ankay Group neglected the proper reconnaissance and flank protection, and the 5th Motorised Rifle Battalion was ambushed at Demidivka by the Soviet mountain rifles of the 96th Mountain Rifles Division. The Hungarians had to stop, dug in, but found them in a critical situation instead of the reinforcements. Lieutenant Colonel Keményfy requested immediate support from his brigade commander. At first Colonel Révhegy's 1st Armoured Cavalry Battalion was called in.

Colonel Révhegyi deployed two tankette companies of his 1st Armoured Cavalry Battalion in the direction of Budy to halt the attacking Russian troops at 13.50 hours on 27 July at Aleksandrovka. During this action, according to memories the commander of the attacking Ansaldos reported to the battalion commander that the terrain is not suitable for the attack, but he was challenged by Colonel Révhegyi as a coward. He replied: "Order confirmed we are going to die"

One tankette company of the 1st Armoured Cavalry Battalion with 18 Ansaldo advanced against the enemy from Gordievka, the wet terrain and the heavy undergrowth blocked the advancing tankettes, the sup-

Lunch break of the Hungarian soldiers belonged to the 3rd Motorised Rifle Battalion, on the right dispatch riders with their Puch motorcycles, on the left a Steyer Baby 50/55 small commander car. [Fortepan/Hajdú Fedő]

Troops resting at a small creek with a temporarily built wooden bridge, on the road is a Ford-Marmon truck visible. [Fortepan/Hajdú Fedő]

Soviet prisoners marching into captivity passing by the advancing Hungarian troops. Some of the Soviet prisoners dressed in civilian clothes, probably military-aged male civilians or freshly recruited soldiers without uniform. [Fortepan/Berkó]

porting bicycle platoon of the 14th Bicycle Battalion under the command of 2nd Lieutenant Zoltán Kékes separated from the tanks. The bogged-down tankette company came under heavy enemy artillery and small arms fire. The engines of the Fiat Ansaldos were prone to stalling. The tankettes' engine had to be restarted manually, from outside of the vehicle. This meant that the driver had to leave the vehicle, even whilst on the battlefield, to try to start the engine. The drivers left the tanks to restart the stopped engines and were killed by infantry and sniper fire. Lieutenant Ferenc Pinezich desperately fired with his twin machine gun of his Ansaldo, when his tankette got a direct mortal hit and killed at Trosztyanec.

Two platoon commanders of the tankette company; Lieutenant Lajos Zomborszky and Ferenc Pinezich were killed. Posthumously they were decorated with the Hungarian Knight Cross with swords.

Out of the 18 attacking tankettes, 12 and their crews were killed in this way. Only one platoon survived because the platoon commander recognized the danger and turned back in time. At the end of the battle, the other company remained six out of the original eleven 35M Fiat Ansaldos. This incident highlighted the poor performance of the Ansaldo in battle and marked the end of its military career.

The 4th Motorised Rifle Battalion followed the attacking Ansaldos and met with the enemy at Trosztyanec. The battalion commander Lieutenant Colonel István Sándor tasked his 1st Company to stop the attacking enemy at Tatarovka-South and with the rest of the battalion repel them. Captain Emil Galett led his 1st Company towards Budy, which was occupied by Soviet troops securing the south flank of their attack. The 1st Company was reinforced with a machine gun platoon under the command of 1st Lieutenant Frigyes Szentkirályi. The machine gunners covered the withdrawing motorized rifles with their 07/31M Schwarzlose machine guns. 1st Lieutenant Szentkirályi ordered his machine gunners to fall back; he was the last to leave the position under heavy enemy fire. He crawled back when his leg was hit by a small arms fire. The young 1st Lieutenant was alone in the no-man land, without help. He started to pull himself on his arms towards the friendly lines. Luckily he was able to cross a road and on the other side, his soldiers noticed and evacuated him to safety. The 4th Motorised Rifles suffered casualties of 13 killed, 34 wounded and 4 missing.

At the same time, the Ankay Group (5th, 6th Motorised rifle, and 13th Bicycle Battalion) engaged with the units of the Soviet 96th Mountain Division south of Gordievka. The soldiers of the 6th Motorised Rifle Battalion fought bravely but under the constant attack of the Soviet mountain, rifles trembled about 14.00 hours South of Gordievka. The two howitzer batteries responsible for the fire support run out of ammunition supply.

Colonel Ankay-Anesini ordered the 11th Light Tank Battalion to counter-attack and clear the situation about

Recovery of a Hungarian Ford-Marmon truck slipped down from the narrow embankment. In front of the Ford-Marmon truck is a 38M Botond all-terrain truck visible. Probably the photo was taken in the rear area because the soldiers not having their weapons. [Fortepan/Hajdú Fedő]

14.45 hours. The heroic charge of the Hungarian light tanks saved the day but caused huge casualties in men and equipment.

At the battle of Gordievka on July 27, the casualty rate of the armored troops was at its highest. During the campaign, eight armored officers were killed, with five of them falling at Gordievka.

1st Lieutenant Ferenc Antalffy served at the 11th Bicycle-Tank Battalion as company commander of the 2nd Company; his Battalion was tasked to attack the Soviet troops at the south part of Gordievka. The light tanks were supported by 1st Lieutenant Endre Szatmáry 2nd Motorised Rifle Company, 6th Motorised rifle Battalion.

The advancing Hungarian light tank company eliminated the enemy resistance without casualties.

Seemingly intact, but abandoned Soviet T-26 light tank on the road facing the advancing Hungarian troops. [Fortepan/Varga dr.]

Reconnaissance troops mounted on mobilized civilian motorbikes advancing in front of the troops. Soldiers are wearing 35M two-piece leather protective suits, and 37M leather crash helmets and goggles armed with 35M rifles and 37M service pistols. [MFI]

Damaged 38M Toldi light tank of the 11th Light Tank Battalion probably after the battle of Gordievka on 27 July 1941. The tank still had the old unit sign, a white lightning bolt of the 1st Reconnaissance Battalion. [Illésfalvi]

Hungarian Hussar squadron riding east in perfect order lead by the squadron commander and his junior officers. [Illésfalvi]

Bicycle platoon cycling their 32M military bicycles, a significant part of their equipment and weapons were attached to the bicycles. [NL-HANA]

A 38M Toldi light tank belonged to the 11th Light Tank Battalion was used for towing a broken-down truck. On the right side of the road a bridge column visible with KV-40 tractors. [NL-HANA]

The Antalffy Company by the own decision of the company commander continued its advance and destroyed an enemy battery and infantry forces. However, they came under the fire of a concealed enemy battery on difficult terrain. 1st Lieutenant Antalffy's light tank was immobilized. He left his Toldi light tank and fought a hand-to-hand battle with his service pistol against the overwhelming enemy forces. He was shot and killed. Posthumously he was decorated with the Hungarian Knight Cross with swords.

1st Lieutenant Endre Szatmári, the company commander of the motorized rifles was also killed in by enemy mortar fire.

Lieutenant András Szotyory's tank platoon also came under heavy enemy artillery fire. Four 38M Toldi light tank was immobilized by artillery fire. Lieutenant Szotyory ordered its crews to fall back. Meanwhile, he led his 38M Toldi tank to flank the Soviet artillery. However his tank was knocked out, his crew was killed. He jumped out with his 9mm service pistol in his hand and was killed by enemy fire. Posthumously he was decorated with the Hungarian Knight Cross with swords.

1st Lieutenant Alfréd Szőke was also killed in action at Gordijevka as the officer of the 11th Bicycle-Tank Battalion. Posthumously he was decorated with the Hungarian Knight Cross with swords. 1st Lieutenant Géza Rováczy was a platoon commander at the 11th Bicycle-Tank Battalion and wounded in action at Gordievka too.

In total the 11th Tank Battalion lost 4 officers and 25 men killed 1 officer and 12 men wounded and 6 men missing in action. The tank battalions lost 19 Toldi light tanks during this battle; most of the tanks were repaired and put back to service.

The relief force of the 13th Bicycle Battalions arrived late afternoon and finally broke the determination of the enemy forces. At the dawn of 28 July, the Soviet forces pulled out of the area.

The 1st Motorised Rifle Brigade started its advance at 10.00 hours that day too according to the plans. By the evening the main forces of the brigade reached their target, Balanovka.

The 2nd Motorised Rifle Brigade suffered the following casualties: 104 dead, 10 missing, 301 wounded and 32 tanks knocked out from 22 to 29 July. The Russians lost 515 killed, with 661 soldiers and 2 tanks, and 23 trucks captured.

The brigades of the Mobile Corps attacked Bersad on 28 July, defended by the remnants of two Soviet divisions. The Hungarians were supported by the German VII Corps from the north and advancing Romanian from the south.

The 3rd Motorised Rifle Battalion came under fire from a hilly position at Bersad, on the River Bug on 29 July. The battalion engaged what was thought to be the enemy and occupied the hill, where they found German troops. This misunderstanding resulted in the deaths of two Hungarian and four German soldiers.

The Hungarian Mobile Corps continued its advance to take part in the operation around Uman to close the encirclement of the Soviet Forces trapped inside the pocket of Uman.

The Hungarian liaison officer subordinated to the German 17th Army, Colonel Sándor Makray had the opinion of providing rest and resupply of the Hungarian troops already fighting without rest in July. However, he stated, that compared with the German casualties and resupply, the Hungarians were in much better condition with fewer casualties than the Germans suffered. As he wrote, the German 4th Mountain Division lost 1200 men in one day during the campaign. On the other hand, of course, the Germans had battle experiences, were better equipped, armed, supplied, and led. For the Hungarian troops as well as for the commanding officers up to the generals, it was the first time since WW1 to be in war.

An uneasy alliance, German, Romanian officers, and a Hungarian captain posing for the camera in a friendly mood. [NL-HANA]

A staged propaganda photo. Destroyed village house and captured Red Army men lead away by Hungarian soldiers. The Hungarian on the left arm with 8mm 31M light machine gun, the leather tool kit of the weapon is on the right hip of the gunner. [War Correspondent Company]

Hungarian rifle squad crossing a creek on a makeshift bridge built from horse-drawn wagons of the supply column. The men carry the metal ammunition boxes for their 31M light machine gun. [War Correspondent Company]

Hungarian 07/31M Schwarzlose machine gun positioning on a hill back to provide covering fire to the advancing riflemen. The platoon commander, a junior officer monitors the terrain with his binocular. [War Correspondent Company]

From Hungary, compensating the losses, fourteen 38M Toldi, nine 39M Csaba, and five 35M Ansaldos were sent to the front by rail on 27 July. However, due to heavy German rail traffic, the vehicles only arrived at Krivoy Rog on 7 October.

The 1st Motorised Rifle Brigade, after two days of street fighting, occupied Pervomaysk on 01 August. The Hungarians lost 40 killed and 100 wounded but captured 500 prisoners, 250 trucks, and 13 anti-tank guns.

As of 1 August, the Mobile Corps was lacking 320 motorcycles, 56 cars, 147 trucks, 20 tractors, 8 armored cars, and 7 light tanks. On 5 August the strength of the armored forces was: 43 serviceable 38M Toldi with the troops plus 14 on flat cars, 14 at the field repair shops, and 24 destroyed or nonrepairable. Out of 57 Csaba armored cars, only 20 were ready for action; 13 were under repair and 20 had been sent back home.

Battle of Uman

The Battle of Uman (15 July – 8 August 1941) was the German offensive operation against the 6th and 12th Soviet Armies – under the command of Lieutenant General I. N. Muzychenko and Major General P. G. Ponedelin, respectively. In the vicinity of Uman, the German forces encircled two Soviet armies, about 25 divisions. The battle occurred during the Kiev defensive operation between the elements of the Red Army's Southwestern Front, retreating from the L'vov salient, and German Army Group South commanded by Field Marshal Gerd von Rundstedt. The Soviet forces were under the overall command of the Southwestern Direction, commanded by Marshal Semyon Budyonny, which included the Southwestern Front commanded by Colonel General Mikhail Kirponos and Southern Front commanded by General Ivan Tyulenev.

By the end of July, after crossing the River Bug, the Mobile Corps reached the Stalin Line at Golovanevsk-Ladyzhynka-Uman. The Hungarian troops began the south cornerstone of the encirclement and were in the position to close the 40-kilometer wide gap on the encirclement around Uman.

On 31 July 1941, the headquarters of the Soviet 17th Rifle Corps was still located in Golovanevsk. Toward the end of the day, the front of G.A. Ponedelin's Group, engulfed by the enemy on nearly all sides, ended up near the Uman region. On 1 August 1941, it was already not possible to come to the help of the troops of the 6th and 12th Armies of the South-West Front, which falling apart at the seams. Units of the 18th Army during the day continued to conduct defensive battles on their own, on a front Kolodistoye-Moshchena-Savran, holding the region of Getmanovka with a single rifle regiment. Under flanking blows of German-Hungarian units, the divisions of the 17th Rifle Corps were forced to retreat to a line Krasnogorka-Moldovka.

The withdrawal of the German Lang group from Golovanevsk was regarded by the Soviet command as a retreat. Around 1900hrs, Soviet units of the 17th Rifle corps broke into the south-eastern and north-eastern quarters of the town. But that penetration was not supported by the remaining corps units, whose attacks were halted by the fierce resistance of jaegers of the 4th Mountain Division. This allowed the Germans to undertake a counterattack with the forces of the LII Corps and the Hungarian Mobile Corps, to consolidate the success, in the evening of 1 August.

Around 2100hrs an order to retreat to Pervomaysk was received. On the same day, General Muzychenko

Advancing motorized rifles riding on a heavily camouflaged 38M Botond all-terrain squad carrier truck. The home-produced Botond trucks prove themselves well during the war. [NL-HANA]

Ambushed Hungarian 39M Ford-Marmon truck, the Soviet forces fired on the truck with small arms the impacts visible on the windshield. [Fortepan/Berkó]

and Ponedelin radioed their status to the STAVAK: *"The situation has become critical. The encirclement of the 6th and 12th Armies is complete. The direct threat of the breakup of the 6th and 12th Armies' combat formation into two isolated segments centered at Babanka and Teklievka region is at hand. There are no reserves. Please clear the way by committing new forces in the Ternovka and Novo-Archangelks sectors. There is no ammunition. Fuel is running out."*

The Hungarian troops advanced deeper into Ukraine, towards the River Bug found the conditions deteriorated and the attitude of the local population more hostile towards them. No built roads existed, the collectivization of the small villages meant that churches

Romanian infantry company leads by an officer marching next to a demolished bridge. The Germans were aware of the tension between the Romanian and Hungarians and separated their area of operation by Italian or German units. [Fortepan/Hajdú Fedő]

Romanian supply column and infantry marching towards the front, contrary to the myth most of the Axis formations marching on foot and field artillery, supply were transported by horse-drawn wagons. [Fortepan/Hajdú Fedő]

Hungarian Composite Bomber Squadron was formed from the Junkers and Caproni bomber aircraft of the 3/II and 4/I Bomber Groups deployed to Sutyska airfield in late July 1941. Junkers Ju 86K-2 bombers of the Composite Bomber Squadron take off for sortie against Soviet targets. [Fortepan/Varga dr.]

Overturned Hungarian Ford truck, belonged to the brigade-level mechanized supply column. The truck transported blankets, clothing for the troop, as well as spare fuel for the truck. [Fortepan/Kokány]

Advancing Hungarian 39M Csaba armored cars around Uman belonged to the Armoured Car Company of the 1st Armoured Cavalry Battalion. The unit sign was painted on the turret over the machine gun port. [NL-HANA]

Heavily camouflaged 39M Csaba armored cars of the 1st Armoured Cavalry Battalion waiting for their marching order. The unit sign was painted on the back of the vehicles too. [NL-HANA]

were used for storage places or animal shelters. The NKVD organized partisan movement was a real threat.

The 1st Motorised Rifle Brigade spearheaded the advancing Mobile Corps, crossing the River Bug at Gaivoron followed by the 2nd Motorised and the 1st Cavalry Brigades on 01 August. The next day at 09.00 hours the 1st Reconnaissance and 1st Motorised Rifle Battalions attacked the heights west of Moldovka. The Soviet forces counter-attacked with 12 light tanks from the village. However, the Hungarian 37mm anti-tank guns and the 20mm turret weapons of the Csaba armored cars knocked out 4 soviet tanks and the rest aborted the attack. Within 30 minutes the Hungarian motorized rifles with the support of the 1st Reconnaissance Battalion captured Moldovka.

Change in command happened on 2 August at the 2nd Motorised Rifle Brigade; Major General János Vörös was replaced by Colonel Ferenc Bissza.

On 2 August 1941, the German 4th Mountain Division split the compressed enemy forces into two parts, near Uman. The German 125th Infantry Division seized the Uman-Novoarkhangelsk road. In the region of Novoarkhangelsk-Oksanino-Dubovaya-Ternovka German aerial reconnaissance established the assembly of 1,400 Soviet cars/wagons preparing for brake trough. The Germans entered Pervomaysk and linked up with the troops of the 17th Army. As a result, two rings of encirclement had formed around Ponedelin's Group.

From the north and east of Novoarkhangelsk units of the 16th, 11th, and 9th Panzer Divisions advanced, as well as the 16th and the "Adolf Hitler" Mechanised Divisions. From the west, the 297th 24th, 125th, and 97th Infantry Divisions approached. To the south, the 1st and 4th Mountain Divisions, the 257th and 96th Infantry Divisions, the 110th and 101st Light Infantry Divisions, and also the units of the Hungarian Corps, Romanian

39M Csaba armored cars of Ensign László Merész, platoon commander at the Armoured Car Company of the 1st Armoured Cavalry Battalion. His platoon stopped and attempted a break trough of the Soviet units on 6 august 1941 at Golovanevsk. [Illésfalvi]

Ambushed Soviet vehicles and dead soldiers lying around the ZIS-5 trucks. The Soviet convoy was struck by air raid or artillery attack. [Fortepan/Hajdú Fedő]

The ambushed Soviet ZIS-5 trucks packed with fuel drums, ammunition, and equipment, the driver and an officer lying dead next to their vehicle. [Fortepan/Hajdú Fedő]

Corps, and an Italian Division were operating. The Italians later occupied Pervomaysk. In all, 22 Axis divisions were operating against Ponedelin's Group, in the region of Pervomaysk, Uman, and Kirovograd.

The Lutwaffe carried out systematic attacks to help annihilate the encircled Soviet troops. The Fliegerkorps IV carried out "rolling aerial attacks" against Red Army units that tried to escape from the trap.

Hungarian soldiers observing the destructed enemy ZIS-5 truck and the fallen Red Army soldiers killed next to their vehicle by small arms fire. [Fortepan/Hajdú Fedő]

The Axis forces could stop the attempted breakthrough of the encircled Red Army units. Knocked out Soviet T-26 flame thrower tank and Soviet soldiers killed in action at the area of Uman in early August 1941. [Fortepan/Album 04]

On 5 August the 1st Motorised Brigade was ensconced in Pervomayks, with several battalions holding the crossings over the River Bug, south of the town. The Hungarians were defending themselves in three directions. The trapped Soviet units frantically tried to break out southwards. The Red Army troops were attempting to withdraw north-eastwards, while the 1st Motorised Rifle and the 1st Cavalry Brigades occupied the only crossing available to the Soviet forces. Finally, the Soviets tried to send in reinforcements from the East to relieve their entrapped troops.

The 1st Cavalry Brigade occupied the River crossings for a length of some 50 kilometers along the northern Riverbank of the Bug. To the north of Pervomayks, the German 101st Light and 257th Infantry Divisions provided flanking cover.

On 5 August about 4000 Soviet soldiers supported by 10 tanks broken through the position of the Ger-

During the clash with enemy forces, Ensign Merész's armored cars destroyed a Red Army motorized rifle company. A shot-out GAZ-AA truck left behind the nearby forest. [Fortepan/Csorba]

Hungarian hussars escorting captured Soviet soldiers, male and female civilians. The prisoners were soon handed over to the Germans, who were responsible for the prisoners of wars, which sealed the fate of most of the prisoners in 1941. [Illésfalvi]

Soviet prisoners of war at Uman guarded by Hungarian hussars on horseback, accompanied by a Captain, squadron commander, and his boyish-looking troop commanders. Interestingly the photo more peaceful than the reality was, with unarmed officers smiling next to the relived-looking Soviet prisoners. [Illésfalvi]

man 4th Mountain Division at Kopenkova and heading towards Golovanevsk. The Hungarian 1st, 2nd Motorised, and 1st Cavalry Brigades were grouped exactly on the path of the attacking Soviet troops. The Cavalry Brigade positioned closest to Soviet units.

On the sunny morning of 6 August, one of the Hungarian signal posts reported to the Corps HQ, that the Soviet forces broke out of the encirclement north of Uman, heavy small arms fire could be heard. According to further reports the Red Army moving around the forests of Golovanevsk alongside the railway line towards the rear echelon of the Hungarian 1st Cavalry Brigade.

The commander of the 1st Cavalry Brigade, Major General Antal Vattay was alarmed by the enemy activity and wanted a clear picture. He tasked a reconnaissance patrol to find and fix the enemy. General Vattay ordered the patrol commander to his HQ and personally briefed him at 08.30 hours to reconnoiter the area around Golovanevsk and swept out the hiding Red Army units, which were located there. The patrol led by Ensign. Ensign László Merész, a young reserve officer belonged to the Armoured Car Company of the 1st Armoured Cavalry Battalion.

On 6 August Ensign László Merész was ordered to carry out a reconnaissance towards the Soviet troops. He had under his command his armored car platoon,

Abandoned Soviet 85mm anti-aircraft gun [Illésfalvi]

three 39M Csaba armored cars, and a bicycle platoon. The plan was to meet the bicycle platoon at a given road junction at Moldovka and proceed together towards the possible enemy positions.

The bicycle platoon was late at the meeting point. Ensign László Merész left one of his armored cars behind to wait for the "rubber hussars" (nickname of the bicycle troops) and continued with his task.

During his movement, he passed the resting staff and the supply columns of the German 257th Infantry Division. The Germans parked alongside the road without any close protection. Ensign Merész while passing while, saluted to the German divisional commander Major General Carl Sachs, who peacefully sitting in his command car.

The two Hungarian armored cars accelerated and drove quickly in the countryside crossing a railway intersection. Suddenly, south of Golovanevsk, they bumped into unidentified cavalry troops. At first, the Ensign Merész identified them as Rumanian troops. He stopped his car and from the turret of his armored car, politely asked the commander in the German language about the situation. Then his second Csaba armored car arrived. Luckily, the driver has spoken Slovakian and was able to identify that the cavalry belonged to the Red Army.

Captured Soviet 76,2mm regimental guns and 45mm anti-tank guns examined by the officers and men of the 4th Hussar Regiment at Uman. [Illésfalvi]

The Hungarian forces captured a significant amount of Soviet weaponry at Uman. Two 76,2mm regimental guns, a 45mm anti-tank gun, limbers, and a DSK heavy machine gun left behind by the Red Army in a small village. [Illésfalvi]

Ensign László Merész immediately ordered his platoon to open fire with their 20mm anti-tank rifles and 8mm machine guns on the advancing Soviet cavalry. It happened so quickly, the Soviet cavalry panicked, dead horses and soldiers covered the roadside. Within a few minutes, two Russian cavalry squadrons were annihilated and beaten back with serious casualties. The Hungarian commander managed to capture two Red Army cavalrymen and brought them back to the German troops for interrogation. The prisoners were questioned with the help of a Slovakian native Hungarian soldier. The prisoners confirmed that their role was to find the gaps on the encirclement to break through back to the Soviet lines. The two advancing Soviet cavalry squadron was followed by a third one. Based on the received information, the 257th German Infantry Division was alerted and their troops prepared for the incoming Russian attack.

More worried-looking Soviet prisoners; soldiers and civilians questioning by a Hungarian officer in a village around Uman in August of 1941. [Illésfalvi]

Soviet prisoners of war, the Hungarians were surprised by the ethnic diversity of the Red Army; however, it reinforced their beliefs of the so-called Asiatic way of fighting methods of the Red Army. [Illésfalvi]

Captured Soviet I-16 fighter plane loaded on a Hungarian Ford truck, a bit overstretched its capacity. [Illésfalvi]

Ensign László Merész reported back on the radio his contact with the enemy to his Brigade Commander. Major General Vattay alarmed his Brigade at 10.30 hours. Ensign Merész did not wait for new orders; he deployed his two armored cars towards the forested area, along the road in an ambush position. Very soon they detected an enemy column of 20 motor vehicles driving south.

The armored cars opened fire at point-blank range. The first Soviet truck was halted by direct hits, the following trucks run into the first one. The 39M Csaba armored cars drove along the road and constantly suppressed the enemy with the anti-tank rifle and machine gunfire. Suddenly, south of the road large number of Soviet infantry advanced from the woods. The Hungarians repelled them with fire and the confused infantry fall back to the forest.

Suddenly two Soviet tanks appeared on the battlefield. The lightly armored cars were no match for the Soviet tanks (probably BT or T-26 tanks). The Hungarian armored cars did not retreat. The 39M Csaba armored cars immediately engaged the hard-skin targets. They opened up the first Soviet tank with their 20mm anti-tank rifles, the Red armored vehicle took a few direct hits and disengaged. By 11.30 Ensign László Merész reported back that they had run out of ammunition and retreat to replenish. Finally, the third armored car and the bicycle platoon arrived, stabilized and sealed the gap, and destroyed the infiltrated Soviet troops.

Hungarian hussar 1st Lieutenant and his sergeant posing with Soviet prisoners of war at Uman. The prisoners still got some kind of food, a rare substance in German captivity. [Illésfalvi]

Soviet prisoners of war under German control marching towards the prisoner camps, the Germans were not prepared and did not care about the huge number of Soviet prisoners lead to starvation and death in the first two years of the war. [Illésfalvi]

During the action, the Hungarian armored cars fired 12.000 machine gun cartridges and 720 20 mm shells. For his leadership and bravery, reserve Ensign László Merész was decorated with the highest Hungarian military decoration for valor, the Officer's Golden Medal for Bravery, and got the Iron Cross from the Germans as well.

According to the interrogated Soviet prisoners, this attempted break trough was lead by the commander of the Soviet 6th Army, General Muzychenko was later taken prisoner; his observation post was just 600 meters from the armored cars of Ensign Merész.

The Germans were lack of combat troops to counter the breaking out Soviet Forces. In the afternoon, reinforcements began to arrive near Golovanevsk.

According to the Soviet sources at 1500hrs, the German 4th Mountain Division/83rd Artillery Regiment dug in on the northern outskirts, a construction company deployed a 1.5 kilometer west, and a company from the

The Hungarians were deeply impressed by the heavy industry of the captured territories. The Steel Factory at Krivoj Rog captured intact. [Fortepan/Varga dr.]

The Steel Factory at Krivoy Rog, the photo was taken from the air by the aircrew of a Hungarian WM-21 Hawk short-range reconnaissance plane. [Fortepan/Varga]

HQ troops of the German LII Corps covered the road from the railway station to the town. Soon, a Hungarian tank company entered the intersection southeast of Golovanevsk. At 1700hrs one heavy field howitzer from the 11th Battery/83rd Artillery Regiment was transferred there.

On 7 August 1941, moving east, the remnant groups of the 190th Soviet Rifle Division engaged several times in minor skirmishes with the enemy, the most important of which was the battle for crossing the Golovanevsk-Pervomaysk road.

The Soviets were forced to surrender at Uman on 08 August; the Germans captured 103.000 prisoners of wars from the 25 divisions, captured or destroyed 317 tanks, 858 artillery pieces, 242 anti-tank and anti-aircraft guns.

General Ponedelin commander of the 12th Army and General Kirillov commander of the 13th Rifle Corps of the 12th Army, both were captured during the Uman

The Steel Factory at Krivoj Rog was captured intact, but the machinery was dismantled by the Soviet workers and evacuated into Siberia to continue the production. [Fortepan/Varga]

Commander of the Hungarian Mobile Corps, Major-General Béla Miklós greeted by a German liaison team. Behind General, Miklós is his chief of staff, staff Colonel Zoltán Zsedényi, between them is a captain, the general's aide du camp. [NL-HANA]

encirclement on 7 August 1941. General Ponedelin was personally interrogated by General Kleist. The generals survived the prison of war camps, were liberated by the Soviets, and after 5 years of extensive investigation were sentenced to death. In 1956 both generals were rehabilitated by the Soviet Military Court.

The 1st Armoured Cavalry Battalion was reorganized before the Battle of Nikolayev. The Battalion took a rest on 8-10 August at Kapitanovka. The reorganized 1st Armoured Cavalry Battalion had a reduced battalion staff, one armored car company, one anti-tank company, and one light tank platoon. The tankette companies, 5 officers and 188 men, and the unserviceable Ansaldo tankettes under the command of 1st Lieutenant Pál Topai were sent to Pervomaysk and later sent back to Hungary. On 21 August Lieutenant Colonel László Bercsényi took over the command of the depleted 1st Armoured Cavalry Battalion from Colonel Ferenc Révhegyi.

Battle of Nikolayev, the last cavalry charge of the Hungarian hussars

After closing the operation at Uman, the demolition of the Soviet 6th and 12th Armies the Axis forces continued their operation. The Germans grouped the German 16th Armoured, 16th Motorised Divisions with the Hungarian Mobile Corps, as Battle Group Kempf to capture Nikolayev. The Germans wanted to prevent the retreating Soviet forces of the 9th Soviet Army and the Coastal Army, to merge.

The Italian Expeditionary Corps (CSIR) also joined in the operation on the Eastern Front in early August 1941. The CSIR consisted of two truck-borne (autotransportable) and one "fast" division. The Germans interpreted these divisions as motorized, what was wishful thinking. However, they were not. The "fast" (celere) divisions had two cavalry one-one motorized artillery and bicycle regiments. The truck-borne division just theoretically was motorized, except the artillery. At best one or two battalions could be transported at the same time by trucks, the rest marched on foot. This severely

The mobility of the Hungarian units strongly relied on the maintenance columns of the Mobile Corps. However, these units were too few and overstretched to keep going the motor vehicles of the troops. Italian-made Fiat Spa Dovunque workshop truck deployed in a factory yard with mechanics work hard. [War Correspondent Company]

Hungarian 38M Toldi light tank belonged to the Field Armoured Battalion, wading through a small creek heading towards the Dnieper. The Field Armoured Battalion was organized from the 9th and 11th Tank Battalions, the field unit insignia consisted of the two former unit's signs, the white triangle and tulip painted on the turret, and the back of the vehicles. [War Correspondent Company]

Advancing motorized rifles belonged to the 1st Motorised Rifle Battalion. Air recognition panels are attached to the engine bonnet of the 38M Botond trucks, the second truck has a lucky horseshoe attached to the grille. Soldiers riding on the mudguard were responsible to detect possible mines planted onto the dirt road. [War Correspondent Company]

During the campaign, the light tank battalions suffered serious losses, although some material and personal replacements were sent, it was not enough. A Field Armoured Battalion was organized based on the 9th and 11th Light Tank Battalions, bearing the unit signs of their original units, the white triangle, and tulip. [War Correspondent Company]

restricted the mobility of the Italians. They were placed between the Hungarian and Romanian troops. The Passubio Division advanced on a parallel line with the Hungarians towards Novaya Odessa.

Facing the Axis offensive was the 18th Soviet Army, 164th Rifle Division commanded by Colonel A. NY. Cservinszkij and the 130th Rifle Division led by Colonel Sz. Sz. Szafronov.

The troops of the Mobile Corps were deployed at Konstantinovka – Voznesensk from 10 to 11 August, where they came under heavy air raids. The Corps lost 14 soldiers killed and 12 armored cars, 2 light tanks, and

Repair and collection point of the broken down Hungarian motor vehicles, at the front is a seriously damaged Krupp Protze anti-tank artillery tractor inspected by an Italian soldier. In the back 39M Ford-Marmon and Ford trucks assembled. [Fortepan/Csorba]

The land tail of the III Short Range Reconnaissance Squadron of the Royal Air Force redeploys towards Krivoj Rog in August of 1941. The troops take a short stop with their Ford fuel truck and an aging Mercedes truck examining a blown-up German tank. [Fortepan/Varga dr.]

Hungarian 40mm 36M Bofors anti-aircraft autocannon deployed at the River Dnieper, covering the Hungarian river defense, but also deployed against land targets. [NL-HANA]

Abandoned Soviet Il-2 ground attack aircraft with collapsed landing gears. The Red Star insignia of the plane is already cut out by souvenir hunters. [Fortepan/Hajdú Fedő]

The airfield of the 1/3 Fighter Squadron of the Royal Air Force at Krivoj Rog was attacked by the Red Air Force in September 1941. Next to the collapsed building is a damaged Ford fuel truck and members of the Squadron. The ensigns wear the Army uniform, while his mate is an Air Force 2nd lieutenant. [Fortepan/Varga dr.]

10 trucks were damaged. Hungarian Air Force fighters shot down 8 Soviet fighters and 4 bombers for the loss of one Hungarian aircraft. According to the Soviet sources, the 96th Soviet Bomber Squadron attacked successfully the Hungarian troops, reporting to destroy 10 enemy armored vehicles and two artillery pieces.

The 1st and 2nd Motorised Rifle Brigades advanced next to each other in the area between the Rivers Bug and Ingul, in a 30-40 kilometer-wide line on 12 August.

On 12 August a reconnaissance patrol of the 1st Reconnaissance Battalion reinforced with a light tank platoon was sent out to explore the roads and bridges around Kaspiro-Nikolajevka. The Hungarian reconnaissance team was attacked by Soviet bombers close to the village of Kaspiro-Nikolajevka. The trucks took cover at the heights in front of the village; the 38M Toldi light tanks looked for shelter in the village. Due to the dust and smoke in the village, the Hungarian armor crew did not notice that Soviet forces occupied Kaspiro-Nikolajevka. The village entrance, the bridge were guarded with two 45mm anti-tank guns. The Hungarian tanks surprised the Soviet gun crew broke into the village and franticly fired on the enemy soldiers. The platoon commander's tank rushed through the village at full speed and lost for one day behind the Soviet line. Finally found another Hungarian patrol and withdrew to the safety. The other two Toldi light tank did not make it, were knocked out in the village.

On 13 August according to Soviet sources, the 2nd Soviet Cavalry Corps' artillery repelled a small Hungarian armored element break trough attempt north of Novaya Odessa.

On 15 August a significant number of Soviet troops broken through led by the 4000 men strong 96th Mountain Rifle Division.

Hungarian fighter squadron equipped with Fiat Cr.42 biplanes lined up at a military airfield. The ground crew prepares the planes ready for takeoff. The yellow identification band is already painted on the fuselage behind the cockpit. [Fortepan/Vargha]

Victory sign painted on the tail of a Hungarian Fiat Cr.42 fighter biplane, the ground crew uses a small star pattern to paint the score, and they also added the date too. [NL-Ha-Na]

The 1st and 2nd Motorised Brigades were able to approach the outskirts of the city by 16 August. The German 16th Armoured Division captured the city on the same day. The Soviets were able to withdraw in time to avoid the encirclements.

During the Battle of Nikolayev the troops, especially the cavalry suffered from the extreme heat, sometimes 40-49 Celsius degrees, lack of water, and burning wheat fields.

The last real cavalry charge of the Hungarian Hussars took place during the battle of Nikolayev on 15 August 1941. The 4/II Hussars distinguished themselves during the operation at Nova-Dancing, Ukraine on 15-16 August 1941. Major Mikecz cavalry combat group hindered the Red Army units from breaking out from the encirclement and thus saved the flank of the German 79th Motorised Infantry Regiment.

The 4th Hussar Regiment was tasked on 15 August by the commander of the 1st Cavalry Brigade to take over the covering of the creek Ingul and be prepared to repel any possible Soviet break trough. Due to the serious illness of the regimental commander, Colonel Géza Erlich, the senior battalion commander Lieutenant Colonel Imre Ireghy took over the command of the regiment before the deployment. It meant that the 4/I Hussar Battalion was commanded by the senior squadron commander Captain Ottmár Szepessy- Schaurek in return. The 4th Hussar Regiment should deploy alongside the main road ready to advance to south and southwest directions. The Hussars moved out their bivouacs at 07.30 hours and reached their assembly areas at Hrisztoforovka at 10.00 hours.

In the first echelon of the 4th Hussars, the 4/II Hussar Battalion was deployed, led by Major Kálmán

Reggiane Re.2000 Falco, the most modern fighter plane of the Hungarian Air Force, was recently purchased from Italy. An experimental Fighter Flight with seven planes under the command of Captain László Gyenes was deployed to the front in 1941. [Fortepan/Vargha]

Mikecz. He already fought as a junior officer during WW1 at the 3rd Hussar Regiment at the K. und K. Armee. He was appointed battalion commander at the 4/II Hussar Battalion in 1941.

The 4/II Hussar Battalion consisted of three squadrons (4/4., 4/5. and 4/6. Cavalry Squadrons) only armed with carbines, light machine guns, and sabers. The Hussar Regiment had a one-one machine gun, anti-tank gun companies, and a cavalry battery to provide heavy weapon support to the mounted squadrons. The 4/II Hussar Battalion was reinforced with three machine gun squads, two anti-tank guns; one horsed artillery battery

Hungarian Re.2000 flight flying in a tight formation, the planes had the yellow-painted engine, fuselage band identification of the Axis aircraft during the Barbarossa Campaign in 1941. [P. Mujzer]

A crash-landed Hungarian WM-21 Hawk short-range reconnaissance plane belonged to the III Short Range Reconnaissance Squadron. [Fortepan/Varga dr.]

Another accident of the WM-21 short-range reconnaissance plane, this one overturned after a failed landing also belonged to the III Short Range Reconnaissance Squadron. [Fortepan/Varga dr.]

(15/31M 75mm guns) and according to German sources four-five 39M Csaba armored cars belonged to the 1st Armoured Cavalry Battalion.

In the second echelon, the 4/I Hussar Battalion was deployed, commanded by Captain Ottmár Szepessy -Schaurek and reinforced with the 4th Cavalry Sapper Squadron, rest of the machine gun company, two anti-tank guns, and the signal platoon

Within 30 minutes the 4th Hussars was tasked to send out a reconnaissance team alongside the railway lines of Nikolayev and check the flank of the German 79th Motorised Infantry Regiment, due to the possible Soviet troop's presence. Major Mikecz's task was to advance towards Mihajlovka – Grejgovo to occupy an area west of the railway line to block any possible movements of the enemy.

The reconnaissance team of the 4/4 Hussar Squadron commanded by Captain Géza Kenéz reinforced with two machine guns and one motorized 37mm anti-tank gun was sent through Marinovka towards Hof Nyemeckij alongside the railway line to explore towards the southwest and west directions.

The monument of the Soviet regime was knocked down either by the locals or the Axis forces. It happened with the statue of Lenin, two fallen soldiers already buried next to the memorial. [Fortepan/Berkó]

Graveyard of Private Pál Vadász was killed in action at Dnepropetrovsk on 29 August 1941; he served at 150th Military Bridge Column. [Fortepan/Berkó]

Knocked and burned out Hungarian KV-40 tractor, used by the anti-aircraft artillery and engineer troops. This vehicle was not popular among the troops; the noisy diesel engine was called a "traitor". [Fortepan/Berkó]

The German 79/I Motorised Infantry Battalion attacked towards Novo-Danzig while the 79/II Motorised Infantry Battalion withdrawing under heavy Soviet pressure at Grejgovo.

The 4/4 Hussar Squadron advanced on horseback under constant enemy fire, took a short stop to readjust the saddles and kits, sending a patrol towards Mihajlovka. The Hussar patrol met a German Panzer Jager Battalion and was informed that Grejgovo was already captured by superior Soviet forces.

The two-point men of the 4th Squadron advanced ahead of their Squadron reached Grejgovo, where Hussars; Mihály Szilvási, and Gyula Német were captured and executed by the Soviet troops. A strange twist in the story, that on the night of 15 August, one of the captured and executed point man, Hussar Gyula Németh, without uniform with serious wounds reported at the Hungarian troops. He explained the 50-60 German prisoners and the two Hungarian Hussars were executed at the village of Grejgovo. His head was injured by several swords blows, lost consciousness. When he regained his consciousness he could sneak out of the heap of his massacred comrades' bodies and reach the friendly troops. The executed German and Hungarian soldiers were found by the advancing cavalrymen of Captain Ottmár Szepessy –Schaurek 4/I Hussar Battalion on 16 August.

The same Hungarian KV-40 artillery tractor belonged to the 150th Military Bridge Column, behind the damaged vehicle the trailer with pontoon visible. [Fortepan/Berkó]

Ensign Pál Berkó, the supply officer of the 150th Military Bridge Column, took a lot of photos of his military life during the war. As a devoted communist he helped a lot of people to survive the war, he made it too. [Fortepan/Berkó]

Half-naked Ensign Berkó posing to the camera, with mobilized civilian cars with air recognition panels and painted white unit sign of the 150th Military Bridge Column. On the right table set for lunch for the reserve officer candidates of the unit. [Fortepan/Berkó]

The 4th Squadron started to advance in wide formation, in two echelons towards Mihajlovka. After 7 kilometer ride, the right-flank platoon commanded by Ensign Sándor Keresztszeghy surprised and charged with hand grenades a Soviet field artillery battery deployed in a valley. Unfortunately, they could not keep the captured enemy guns because they were evicted by superior Soviet forces. The platoon commander, Ensign Keresztszeghy wounded seriously while leading his men.

The rest of the Hussars also dismounted to organize an attack against the Soviet forces. However, a battalion of strong enemies assembles at the boundary line to attack the Hungarian hussars. When the Soviet attackers approached the Hussars 200 meters away, the squadron commander Captain Kenéz ordered his troops to mount and disengage the Soviet troops. The Hungarian Hussars mounted on their horses under heavy artillery and mortar barrage. Captain Géza Kenéz was mortally wounded right after ordering his troops to withdraw. The command of the 4/4 Squadron was taken over by reserve 1st Lieutenant István Nászay, the deputy squadron commander, led the troops to fall back in a full gallop towards the advancing 4/II Hussar Battalion.

While the reconnaissance team fought desperately, the 4th Hussar Regiment already started his advance at 12.30 hours. The Hussar regimental commander with his tactical HQ joined the German 79th Motorised Infantry Regiment HQ at Marynivka. Based on the German situation report Lieutenant Imre Ireghy tasked his first echelon to attack towards Mihajlovka- Grejgovo and take a position 4 kilometers west of the railway line. The

The catering team of the 150th Military Bridge Column deployed at Dnepropetrovsk in late August 1941. The field kitchen was transported by a Ford truck with food stocks and kitchen equipment. [Fortepan/Berkó]

The catering team moved into a yard of a workshop in Dnepropetrovsk, to hide from the aerial observation of the Red Air Force. The fresh cabbages were locally acquired by the requisitioning teams made up of the men of the supply column to provide fresh food for the troops. [Fortepan/Berkó]

German Pz.IVF-1 medium tank passing the trailer of the Hungarian 150th Military Bridge Column. The Pz.IV had a small letter tactical number 332 painted on the turret. [Fortepan/Berkó]

area of operation was a huge, open wheat field, partially burning with limited visibility.

Major Mikecz stopped and reorganized the 4th Squadron and ordered a charge right away. The cavalry squadrons of the 4/II Hussar Battalion formed into attack formation, sabers in hand, and started to gallop towards the Red Army positions. The unit was led by Major Mikecz in front of his hussars. The cavalry was supported by 4-5 Csaba armored cars on the flanks. The Hungarians were under artillery and infantry fire.

German motorized column waiting for river crossing, German field police regulate the traffic on the bridge at Dnepropetrovsk. Soviet civilian refugees with their belongings escape from the war zone. [Fortepan/Berkó]

Axis forces meeting at Dnepropetrovsk, at the bombed house two Italian soldiers resting, another on the right marching towards the bridge. On the left, a German dispatch rider is visible with three smoking Hungarian officers dressed in leather coats. [Fortepan/Berkó]

As the hussars approached the Soviet units, the intensity of the enemy fire started to decrease. The morale of the enemy was broken and the defense collapsed.

During the attack, one of the Hungarian anti-tank gun crew, led by Corporal János Maczkó spotted two Soviet fighter planes preparing for the taking off behind the advancing Soviet troops. Corporal Maczkó ordered his gun crew into action and with three shots destroyed one of the planes, the other escaped.

This event was captured by a German war journalist Erich Kern, who served at the elite Leibstandarte SS Adolf Hitler Brigade, recounted the event in his book, Der Grosses Rauch. *"German troops were pinned down behind a railway embankment by strong Red Army forces. German infantry attacked four times but was repulsed each time by superior forces. The battalion commander cursed and tried to push his men into a new attack in vain, as the Russians steadily held their positions. It was then, when instead of the artillery barrage we were repeatedly asking for, that Hungarian cavalry squadrons showed up. We were laughing. What do these guys want to do here with their sleek horses, armed only with swords? Suddenly we were taken with astonishment. These Hungarians made mad! Squadrons followed others coming from our rear. Following a loud command, the hussars drew their swords and charged the enemy, virtually glued to their horses, with the metal blades of the swords shining in the sun. They were led by a middle-aged, sword-swinging colonel, with silver rank insignia sparkling on his uniform's collar. Several light armoured cars covered the flanks ... Forgetting the immediate danger, we stood up and watched the unbelievable scene. It looked like an extraordinary cavalry movie. The Russian fired at their unlikely attackers, but shots became more sporadic and finally ceased. We watched in astonishment how the Soviet battalion, which thus far fanatically defended its position, panicked and hastily retreated under the pressure of the charging cavalry. The Hungarians savoring their success*

Brothers in arms at Dnepropetrovsk, an Italian Bersaglieri surrounded by two Hungarians, on the left an officer candidate sergeant, on the right is a 2nd Lieutenant. [Fortepan/Berkó]

The German engineers deposited wood beams to reinforce or rebuilt the pontoon bridge in case of any damage. At that point, the River Dnieper was a few kilometers wide. [Fortepan/Berkó]

Soviet prisoners of war pressed into carrying German ammunition boxes at Dnepropetrovsk, next to the pontoon bridge built by the Germans in September 1941. [Fortepan/Berkó]

German pontoon bridge leading from the city to the other side of the River Dnieper. Axis troops cross the bridge, Soviet prisoners carrying ammunition. On the left a German staff car and an Italian Autocaretta small truck are visible. [Fortepan/Berkó]

cut the running soldiers down with their swords. This time, incredibly, ancient weapons and war techniques triumphed over modern technology ".

The Hussars stabilized the front line, connected with the forces of the German 79th Motorised Infantry regiment. The 1st Horsed Artillery Battalion also arrived, but just went into firing position the next morning.

On 16 August the German and Hungarian forces continued their attacks and broke the resistance of the Soviet Forces and occupy the valley of River Ingul. Later that day the 3rd Motorised Artillery Battalion of the Hungarian Hussars went in firing position west of Mihajlovka to support the troops.

Major Kálmán Mikecz was promoted to Lieutenant Colonel in 1941 and for his action, he was awarded the Hungarian Knight Cross.

During the two-day-long battle, the 4th Hussar Regiment lost one officer, six hussars killed in action, two officers and 24 hussars wounded, 4 hussars missing in action, 14 horses lost too. The Hussars captured 175 Soviet prisoners, three tanks, two armored cars, two anti-tank guns, one anti-aircraft gun, six trucks, and one aircraft.

The Battle of Nikolayev ended on 17 August, majority of the Soviet forces were able to avoid being destroyed. The Hungarian mobile troops were allowed a brief period of rest between 17-27 August, to recuperate following the long advance. The constant lack of fuel also hampered the movements of the troops. The Mobile Corps had to reach the movement readiness by 27 August to deploy from Krivoy Rog to the Dnieper.

River defense at the Dnieper

On 18 August the NKVD blew a 120-meter wide hole in the dam of the Dnieper Hydroelectric Dam. The wave of several dozes meters of high water swept away

Downtown of Dniepro occupied by the Axis forces, with a white stone fountain and the majestic but burned down building recalls a prosperous life in the past. [Fortepan/Berkó]

Captured Soviet ammunition, 120mm mortar shells, and aviation bombs packed into the wooden frame. [Illésfalvi]

Rail Way Bridge at Dnepropetrovsk was blown up by the Soviet forces during the siege of the city. It was a specially built two stories railway bridge. [Fortepan/Berkó]

The demolition charges only destroyed just a part of the bridge provided an opportunity for the Axis to rebuild this important bridge for them. [Fortepan/Berkó]

everything situated in the floodplain of the Dnieper, locals, refugees, soldiers.

The Soviet Force's main goal was to cover the evacuation of the factories, especially in the lower Dnieper River and Donbas region in Ukraine. The stubborn defense of the Soviet Southwestern Front paid dividends. The Germans were blocked to strengthen their troops advancing towards Moscow and providing time for dismantling factories' machinery to evacuate them out of reach of the Germans to Siberia.

The 1st German Panzer Group established a bridgehead at Dnepropetrovsk on the River of Dnieper on 26 August. South from this point, two German divisions screened the Riverbank, to replace them the Hungarian Mobile Corps was called in. The Hungarians were assigned the mission of guarding the southern flanks of the Army Group South.

On the Soviet side, the South Front forces challenged the Hungarian troops. The Soviet 12th Army, commanded by Major General I. V. Galanyin, had

According to the personal memoirs of the men, after the mere survival of the campaign, the next important issue was the food. Hungarian soldiers making their meals were probably chickens liberated from a Soviet agricultural cooperative. [Fortepan/Kokány]

Hungarian patrol monitoring the east side of the river bank at the Dnieper, the Hungarians was responsible for river defense and covering the flank of the German units fighting at Dnepropetrovsk. [War Correspondent Company]

The blocking position of the Hungarian motorized rifles consisted of a 37mm 36M (Pak 36) anti-tank gun covered by a rifle squad armed with a 31M light machine gun and 35M rifles. Each metal box contains five spare magazines for the light machine gun. The troops were already dressed in greatcoats because the weather was cool in mid-September. [HIM]

the 270th 274th Rifle, 11th Tank Divisions, 268th, 374th Artillery Regiments faced the Hungarian 2nd Motorised Rifle Brigade and the Ankay Group. The 18th Soviet Army was commanded by General Smirnov17th and 55th Rifle Corps, 96th Mountain Rifle, 130th, 164th, 169thRifle, and 30th Cavalry Divisions, 437th Artillery, and 82nd Anti Aircraft Artillery Regiments. The 96th Mountain Rifle 30th Cavalry Division and the 437th Artillery Regiment opposed the 1st Motorised Rifle Brigade at Nikopol.

Due to the demolished dam at Zaporozhe, the water level of the Dnieper was reduced by 10 meters. In some parts of the river, it could be crossed on foot. The strong vegetation in the floodplain, islands, and sandbanks were ideal hiding places and infiltration points for the Soviet troops.

The Hungarians were given a front 200 kilometers long, but they were too weak to set up a rigid defense. The commander of the Mobile Corps organized a token

The Hungarian defense line was sporadic, consisted of observation posts manned by half squads armed with 35M rifles and 31M light machine guns. [Fortepan/ Kokány]

Hungarian machine gun team armed with 8mm 07/31M Schwarzlose machine gun with distinctive flash hider. The Hungarians dug in the edge of the riverbank, facing the East side of the river with the industrial complex of Dnepropetrovsk. [War Correspondent Company]

The large Railway Bridge over the River Dnieper at Dnepropetrovsk was also rebuilt by the Hungarian engineer and railway construction troops. [War Correspondent Company]

The vehicles and howitzers of the 2nd Light Howitzer Battalion of the 2nd Motorised Rifle Brigade crossing the River Dnieper at Dnepropetrovsk. The unit sign white heart shot by arrow painted on the howitzer shield as well as on the back of the 38M Botond truck. [War Correspondent Company]

defense alongside the River to monitor the Soviet activities. The dismounted bicycle, cavalry, and motorized rifle troops occupied the strongholds along the River and the motorized and armored troops acted as the mobile reserve. At the front line, the field posts were located 800-3000 meters apart from each other. Daytime the areas between the field posts are controlled by visual observation and patrolling. At night time the troops tried to control the lines with listening and patrolling. The gaps between the positions were sporadically blocked by anti-personal mines.

The 2nd Motorised Brigade was assigned to a 55-kilometer long defense line, which included the Island of Khortytsia situated in front of Zaporozhe. The 2nd Motorised Rifle Brigade had 6 battalions and 14 batteries. The artillery grouped behind the 2nd Motorised Rifle Brigade was reinforced with the an additional motorised howitzer battalion and corps level medium artillery batteries too.

The 1st Motorised Rifle Brigade with 3 battalions and 4 batteries was in defense south of the 2nd Motorised Rifle Brigade alongside the 100-kilometer long Riverbank. The Ankay Group, commanded by Colonel Győző Ankay-Anesi consisted of the 13th, 14th Bicycle Battalions, 1st Armoured Cavalry Battalion, two Bofors

The Hungarian 105th Railway Construction Company rebuilt the Railway Bridge over the River Mokra at Zaporozhe. The steam locomotives are testing the rebuilt bridge. [Fortepan/Varga dr.]

batteries, two anti-tank companies, and the 3rd Motorised Artillery Battalion were assigned to a 45-kilometer long defense line north of the Island of Khortytsia. Two cavalry battalions (mounted) were kept in reserve at Tomakovka, but the rest of the cavalry troops were dismounted and dispersed among the rifle units along the Riverbank. The Mobile Corps tactical HQ is also located at Tomakovka.

The most critical point of the defense was the island of Khortytsia opposite the city of Zaporozhe, it was 12 kilometers long and 1,5-2 kilometers wide crossed by the railway line. The Soviet forces were determined to keep their position until the factories were dismantled and withdraw back to the Soviet Union.

The Hungarian 5th Motorised Rifle and the 12th Bicycle Battalions replaced the German units on the island on 29-30 July. The 8-kilometer long defense line of the 5th Motorised Rifle Battalion was manned by two and a half rifle companies; one-half the companies were kept in reserve. The Hungarians were supported by two light and on medium artillery batteries.

The density of the river defense was weak, sporadic elsewhere too. For example the 2nd Company of the 13th Bicycle Battalion taken over a 12-kilometer sector with four platoons armed with 11 light machine guns and one anti-tank rifle.

By 1 September 1941, the Hungarian troops took over the whole sector from the Germans. Already on the evening of 1 September at the south-east part of the island of Khortytsia Soviet troops infiltrated the island and at 22.00 hours clashed with the 2nd Rifle Company of the Hungarian 5th Motorised Rifle Battalion. The skirmishes lasted until midnight

The next day the hostilities continued on the island, the Hungarian motorized rifles repelled the attack killed 12 and captured 11 Soviet soldiers. They were over-aged 40-45 years old reservists, belonged to the 965th Soviet Rifle Regiment/ 274th Rifle Division.

The next day the pressure of the Soviet forces grown step by step, the Hungarian heavy weapons are broken down due to the extreme use, the junior officer reported that the men were exhausted by the nonstop enemy activity.

The defense sector of the 1st Motorised Rifle Brigade was under air raids and artillery barrage of the Soviet 437th Corps Artillery Regiment on 3 September. When the artillery preparation ended forces of Colonel Shepetov 96th Mountain Rifle Division tried to cross the River in small wooden boats. The Hungarian troops reacted with concentrated small arms and artillery fire, 7-8 Soviet barge toppled the rest turned back.

At 00.30 on 5 September, under heavy artillery preparation, a strong force of Soviet troops attacked the defense position of the 5th Motorised Rifle and the 12th Bicycle Battalion at Zaporozhe. At 17.00 hours the defense line of the 1st Company/5th Motorised Rifle Battalion was broken by the enemy. The combat became heavy and wavering between the Hungarian and Soviet troops on the island. The brigade commander Colonel Ferenc Bissza mobilized all of its reserves, the 6th Motorised Rifle, and 14th Bicycle Battalions, to relieve the Hungarian troops at Khortytsia.

Another view of the rebuilt bridge over the River Mokra at Zaporozhe. The Hungarian 105th Railway Construction Company x-shaped metal frames to rebuild the bridge. [Fortepan/Varga dr.]

The commander of the Mobile Corps requested permission from the 1st German Armoured Group to withdraw from the island of Khortytsia. The Germans refused it and provided German troops to replace the 1st Hungarian Motorised Rifle Brigade, which in return could strengthen the defense at Khortytsia. Major General Béla Miklós categorically forbade the evacuation of the Hungarian position.

The situation further deteriorated on 6 July at the island of Khortytsia. The Group commander, Colonel Antal Benda finally ordered the withdrawal of the Hungarian troops from Khortytsia on the bridge and ferries to the western side of the River Dnieper. Meanwhile, the 14th Bicycle Battalion dashed to the island by the bridge to take a bridgehaead and cover the withdrawing troops. The sappers also prepared the bridge over the Dnieper for demolition.

The 5th Motorised Rifle Battalion suffered 2 officers, 23 men killed, 9 officers and 166 men wounded and 52 men missing in action.

Colonel-General Kleist was upset due to the evacuation, which went against his order, requested investigation and punishment of the Hungarian commander in charge. The investigation concluded that the evacuation from Khortytsia was caused by the overwhelming Soviet forces and the Hungarian forces were exhausted too.

The 1st Motorised Rifle Battalion attacked on 6 September the units of the 96th Mountain Rifle Division and the 127th and 138th Cavalry Regiments of the 30th Cavalry Division logged south of Nowo Kijewka. The Soviet units were supported by the gunboats of the Dniepr River Flotilla. The depleted Hungarian motorized rifles were reinforced with one tank platoon of the 9th Tank Battalion, the Brigade's Movement Control Company. The Hungarian troops desperately charged the Soviet positions. One Hungarian anti-tank company advanced and firing from a point-blank range at the Soviet troops, the 38M Toldi light tanks flanked the enemy. Finally, the men of the Movement Control and the Motorised Rifle Companies broke the resistance of the Soviet troops in hand-to-hand combat. By 11.00 hours the Riverbank was cleared from the Red Army troops, 5 Soviet officers and 120 enlisted men were killed and 120 men were captured.

The 16th German Motorised Division started to replace the troops of the 1st Motorised Rifle Brigade on 6 September.

The defense positions were reorganized, normal defense sectors were allocated to the Motorised Rifle Brigades. Each brigade had one motorized rifle battalion, one movement control company, and 15 light tanks with one day fuel in reserve. Each battalion in defense position was supported by one light howitzer battery. A central artillery support group and a long-rang artillery battery was organized. Parallel to the River concealed Bofors guns were installed to provide flanking fire.

Later on, in return the Hungarians also infiltrated the island of Khortytsia in section/ platoon strength capturing prisoners, collecting information.

On 17 September the Soviet troops tried to cross the river at several points repelled by the concentrated fire of the 1st and 2nd Motorised Rifle Brigades. The

The autumn rain made the roads impassable for the troops; just the light tanks and the38M Botond trucks could negotiate the calf-deep muddy roads. A 38M Botond all-terrain truck tows a trailer towards Mechebelovka. [Fortepan/Csorba]

Hungarian observed that the Soviet boats which tried to return to the friendly side of the River were fired upon by the Soviet NKVD teams.

19 September, the staff officers of the Mobile Corps and the Italian "Torino" Division discussed the possibilities of the take over the Hungarian positions by the Italians.

The troops of the Southwest Front were encircled by the German 1st Armoured Group from the south and the 2nd Armoured Group from the north, on 19 September the Germans entered Kiev. The pressure on the Hungarian forces alongside the River Dnieper reduced. Island Khortytsia was also evacuated by the Soviets and captured by the German 4th Guard Regiment.

The operation at the Dnieper ended on 6 October. The Hungarians lost 9 officers, 148 men killed, 54 officers and 762 men wounded, 74 men missing in action. To compensate for the loss, the II and VII Bicycle Battalions were deployed and subordinated to the 2nd Motorised Rifle and 1st Cavalry Brigades. The 11th and 9th Tank Battalion was withdrawn and sent home, its remaining light tanks and vehicles were regrouped to the Armoured Field Battalion.

On the Soviet side, the estimated losses were 3000 killed and 3000 wounded officers and men.

Advance towards Izyum

From 27 September to 11 October, the Mobile Corps received a respite from the fighting to reorganize and recover, in an area south of Tomakovka. On 10 October the cavalry components of the Cavalry Brigade were sent home. At this time the Corps had only two weak motorized rifle brigades, without bicycle battalions or reinforcements. The bicycle battalions had been sent to the rear areas. In September each light tank battalion had only one company of 38M Toldi tanks. The troops had 35-40 armored vehicles, which were organized into one Armoured Field battalion based around the 1st Armoured Cavalry Battalion.

The units of the motorized rifle brigades were reorganized with three motorized rifles one reconnaissance battalions, signal, sapper companies, light artillery batteries, and allocated light tanks. At the motorized rifle battalions,' one rifle company was disbanded, the personnel was distributed among the other companies to compensate for the losses. The heavy and automatic weapons of the battalions remained at the reduced strength units, so their firepower did not change. The surplus 38M Botond vehicles were allocated to the artillery battalions and supply column of the brigades.

The second echelon of the brigades consisted of the bicycle battalions, medium artillery batteries, and the rest of the supply column.

The different units of the brigades were organized into combat groups were based on the various motorized rifle battalions, reinforced with engineer, artillery, and A/A troops. The 1st Motorised Rifle Brigade had three combat groups and two reconnaissance subgroups. Necessity dictated that the light tanks be shared among the combat and reconnaissance groups. Although the light tanks were useless against well-organized and concentrated anti-tank fire, they were very quick and therefore useful as a surprise element during battle. At the 1st Motorised Rifle Brigade, 10-10 x 38M Toldi tanks were assigned to each of two combat groups, while 5 light tanks were assigned to one of the reconnaissance subgroups.

The Mobile Corps was subordinated to General Viktor von Schwendler's Battle Group, under the Ger-

In October the rainy weather practically stopped the advancing troops of the Mobile Corps. Vehicles of the 1st Reconnaissance Battalion; Ford-Marmon truck with ex-Polish fuel trailer, 39M Csaba armored car, behind them a 38M Botond truck, and a local panje wagon. [War Correspondent Company]

man 17th Army to attack and occupy the Doneck Basis. The Germans wanted to conquer one of the biggest industrial areas of the Soviet Union, with coal mines, steel factories vital for performing the war.

The Hungarian troops were responsible to protect the left flank of the Schwendler's Battle Group and started their advance on 11 October. The Hungarians aimed to capture the town of Izyum and further to take Kupjanszk and finally reach Kharkov. However, this aim was unrealistic, the weather turned against the attacking Axis forces. The autumn, the rainy season started on 7 October with pouring rain which turned the roads into impassable mud fields. Later sleet and snow started to fall. On a high military-political level the Hungarians interceded at the Germans to relieve the troops of the Mobile Corps and sent the troops back to Hungary.

Beginning 17 October, the motorized troops advanced towards Izyum. Due to the difficult weather conditions, the motorized rifle battalions of the 2nd Motorised Rifle Brigades were stuck in the muddy road on 19 October. However, the new commander of the German 17th Army, General Hermann Hoth officially thanked Major General Béla Miklós for the excellent movement achievement of the Hungarian troops.

On 27 October, Major General Béla Miklós flew back to Budapest to discuss the road map of the withdrawal; Major General Jenő Major was the acting Corps Commander.

The combat groups of the 1st Motorised Rifle Brigade, after heavy fighting, penetrated Mecsebelovka. The defending Russian troops counter-attacked, but the commander of the Brigade deployed his light tanks in a successful action against the Soviet infantry. The Hungarians suffered light losses, in return 300 Soviet soldiers were captured. The Hungarians pursued the withdrawing Soviet troops and captured another 700 prisoners of war.

During this fighting Lieutenant, Győző Laczkó was killed in action on 20 October. He was sent to the front as a replacement in August 1941, to take over the platoon commander position at the 4th Company 9th Bicycle-Tank Battalion. Later he was transferred as platoon commander to the Field Armoured Battalion fighting at Mecsebelovka when his Toldi tank's turret was shot at close range by a Soviet anti-tank gun. He was posthumously he was promoted to 1st Lieutenant and decorated with the Hungarian Knight Cross with swords.

1st Lieutenant István Locskay was posted to the 1st Reconnaissance Battalion from his original unit, from the II Bicycle Battalion on the front, mortally wounded at Mecsebelovka on 20 October 1941, during the heavy street fighting buried at Otdohnina, 21 October 1941. Posthumously he was promoted to Captain and decorated with the Hungarian Knight Cross with swords.

The Hungarian forces reached the River Donets at Izyum -South on 28-29 October.

On 2 November the reconnaissance patrols of the 1st Motorised rifle Brigade entered Izyum and clashed with the Soviet rearguards.

On 4 November the 2nd Motorised Rifle Brigade encircled and destroyed a group of Cossack cavalry and partisans in a forest of Bogorodicsnoje and captured a huge quantity of food and ammunition. Food was the real precious catch because the food supply was sporadic.

According to the further German plans the Hungarian Mobile Corps was tasked to take Konstantinovka and later reach Vorosilovgrad. However, Major General Béla Miklós returned from Budapest on 11 November and informed the Germans that the Hungarian Mobile Corps in accordance with the OKH permission would be relived and regrouped for redeployment to its home garrisons as soon as possible.

Hungarian Royal Air Force during the operation in Ukraine

According to the condition of the Peace Treaty; any military-related aviation, training, producing, or purchasing military aircraft were prohibited for the Hungarians. However, from the beginning, the importance of the Air Force in a future conflict was evident for the Army High Command. Already in the early 20s pilot training started under the cover of civilian flying schools.

In 1924, within the Ministry of Trade, the Aviation Authority was established, as the cover command institute of the future Air Force. The Allied supervision was eased but the financial state of Hungary did not allow any significant improvement by that time. The Hungarians could purchase some outdated British, Italian, and German trainer planes.

The Weiss Manfred Factory was interested in purchasing the license right off the Udet U12/12a and Heinkel HD22 planes. The Dutch Fokker Factory also offered planes to the Hungarians, the Fokker C.V. two-seater general-purpose aircraft, and the twin-engine F.VIII passenger planes.

The secret Hungarian Air Force had nine air squadrons with a mix of old and non-military planes keep the elementary training on until the end of the 20s.

By the early 30s the Air Force got its distinctive uniform, although the units were still working under the covert title; like aerial photo section, weather forecast unit, etc.

In the early 30s, due to the friendly Italian-Hungarian connection, the Hungarians were able to purchase Fiat Cr.20 fighters and in 1936 Caproni Ca.101 bombers, the first real warplanes since the WW1.

In 1935 the Hungarians ordered a significant quantity of military aircraft from Italy and Germany to build up the Royal Hungarian Air Force. Seventy-six Fiat Cr.32 fighter biplanes, sisty-six Junkers Ju 86K-2 bombers, forty-six Heinkel He 46E-2 short-range, and eighteen He 70K long-range reconnaissance planes arrived in Hungary.

By 1937 the Royal Hungarian Air Force had 255 military aircraft organized into 25 air squadrons. The fighters were organized into the 1st Fighter Regiment with two fighter groups, each had three squadrons. The bomber force consisted of two bomber regiments with seven bomber squadrons equipped with Junkers Ju 86K-2 bombers and two squadrons equipped with Caproni Ca.101 night bombers. The Heinkel He 46E-2 short-range reconnaissance planes served in seven corps subordinated reconnaissance squadrons. The Heinkel He70K planes belonged to the 1st Independent Long-range Reconnaissance Group with two squadrons.

In 1937, the Weiss Manfred Factory based on the Fokker C.V. aircraft developed a conventional biplane with fixed undercarriages, the WM-21 Hawk short-range reconnaissance/ army cooperation aircraft. Thirty-six WM-21 was ordered by the Hungarians in 1938.

After the signature of the Bled Agreement, the clandestine status of the Air Force changed, it was named officially as the Royal Hungarian Honvéd Air Force. The new military insignia, the red-white-green chevron was painted on the planes as well as with the military code letters; V- vadász(fighter), B- bombázó (bomber), F- felderítő (reconnaissance), G- gyakorló (trainer), and I-iskola (school).

The air squadrons of the Royal Hungarian Air Force were mobilized and deployed during the operation connected to the enlargement of Hungary from November 1938 until April 1941.

In 1938, the Hungarian aircrew especially the fighter pilots flew their Fiat biplanes for at least two years period knowing their planes and their comrades well. The Junkers bombers just arrived in the spring of 1938, leaving less time for the crew to practice with their bombers.

During the so called "small war" between Hungary and Slovakia, the Royal Hungarian Air Force was babtised in fire. Nine Slovakian planes were shot down by the Hungarian Fiat Cr.32 fighter biplanes and two Slovakian planes collided destroying the aircraft and the crew. Ten Slovakian planes were damaged by the Hungarian airstrike at the airfield of Igló during the conflict.

In 1939, due to the Italian governmental credit, the Hungarians ordered fifty Fiat Cr.42 biplane and seventy Reggiane Re.2000 Falco fighters. The Re.2000 was a modern aircraft with retractable undercarriage, mono winged, closed cockpit, but was less easy to fly causing accidents among the pilots. The Hungarians also purchased thirty-six Caproni Ca.135bis bombers from Italy to equip a bomber group. The Re.2000 and Ca.135bis planes were deployable by the summer of 1941.

The Royal Hungarian Air Force had 2 fighters, 2 bomber, 1 short-range reconnaissance regiments, 1 long-range reconnaissance group, and 1 paratrooper battalion in 1941.

The Hungarian Air Force mobilized the 1st Aviation Brigade to support the 3rd Hungarian Army during the Yugoslavian Campaign, commanded by Colonel István Bánfalvy. The Brigade consisted of the 1st and 2nd Fighter Regiments with two-two fighter groups equipped with Fiat Cr.32 and Fiat Cr.42 fighter biplanes, the 4th Bomber Regiment with two groups, and 3/5 Bomber Squadron with Junkers Ju 86K2 bombers. The 1st Independent Long-Range Reconnaissance Group with Heinkel He 70K planes and short-range reconnaissance squadrons subordinated to the Army Corps. The 1st Independent Paratrooper Battalion was also put on standby.

The Hungarian Air Force lost two-two Fiat Cr.32 and Fiat Cr.42 fighters, one –one WM-21 short-range reconnaissance, and S.M. 75 transport planes due to accidents. Another two Fiat Cr.32 and one Fiat Cr.42 fighters were damaged. In return one – one Yugoslavian Blenheim, Dornier Do 17K and S.M. 79B planes were captured intact by the Hungarians.

In the summer of 1941, the order of battle of the Royal Hungarian Air Force did not change. However, the new Caproni Ca.135bis and Reggiane Re.2000 planes were delivered to the combat squadrons.

At the request of Germany, similarly to the designated land forces, the Royal Hungarian Air Force's units were mobilized of north-eastern Hungary on June 14, 1941. Some of the fighter squadrons were standing by at the military airports of Miskolc and Huszt. Bomber units relocated from Transdanubia to the Debrecen region to stand by in case of action.

On the afternoon of 26 June, right after the bombing raid on Kassa, the Royal Hungarian Air Force carried out a reconnaissance sortie over Stryi, Stanislav, and Kolomea by a Heinkel He 70K plane to explore enemy positions. In the early stage of the operation, the aviation units were commanded and controlled by the 1st Aviation Brigade deployed to Huszt.

The Army Command ordered a retaliation strike on 27 June against Soviet land targets alongside the border. The raid was carried out by sixteen Junker Ju 86K-2 bombers of the 4/II Bomber Group, eight Caproni Ca.135bis planes of the 3/5 Bomber Squadron and a few additional Junker Ju 86K-2 bombers 4/I Bomber Group escorted by nine Fiat Cr.42 fighters of the 2/3 Fighter Squadron against Stanislav.

One of the Hungarian Fiat Cr.42 flew by Ensign László Kázár strafed land targets when was hit by Soviet anti-aircraft cannon at Kuty. He crash-landed behind the enemy lines, set fire his plane, and with the help of the Ukrainian civilians hiding in the woods until 13 July, when he met with Romanian troops.

The VIII and X Short-range Reconnaissance Squadrons hit the targets alongside the borderline, strafing and bombing Soviet positions. The VIII Squadron was led by Captain Árpád Platthy.

On 29 June, twenty-five Hungarian Ju 86K-2 and Ca.135bis bombers escorted by Fiat Cr.42 fighters attacked Styrj, met heavy enemy anti-aircraft fire.

The first casualties of the Hungarian Air Force were pilot Ensign István Sallai and observer 1st Lieutenant László Bánya of the X Short-range Reconnaissance Squadron missing in action at Zielona, their WM-21 Hawk reconnaissance plane F.242 was shot down by the Soviet anti-aircraft artillery on 29 June. On the same day, the Fiat Cr.42 fighters of the 2/3 Fighter Squadron led by Captain Aladár Szobránczy clashed with seven Soviet SB-2 bombers attacking the Railway Station of Chop. The Hungarian fighters shot down three Soviet bombers without losses.

Aviation Group was formed to support the Hungarian land forces, commanded by Lieutenant Colonel Béla Orosz, at the beginning only consisted of the 2/3 Fighter and VII and X Short-range Reconnaissance Squadrons. Later the 4th Bomber Regiment, 3/5 Bomber Squadron, and the 1/1st Long-range Reconnaissance Squadron added to the formation.

In August an Experimental Fighter Flight commanded by Captain László Gyenes, of the 1/2 Fighter Squadron equipped with seven Reggiane Re.2000 fighter planes deployed to the front, to gain experiences with the new fighters.

On 04 July one Heinkel He 70K plane, F.401 of the 1/1st Long-range Reconnaissance Squadron carried out a reconnaissance sortie over Kamenyec-Podolszk. The Hungarian plane was attacked by three Soviet I-16 fighter planes. The gunner franticly fired with his single 8mm machine gun, the plane was hit a lot of times, caught fire in the air, and crashed. The crew; 2nd Lieutenant Sándor Fülöp observer, Sergeant Márton Várhalmi pilot and Lance corporal Ferenc Rusznák radio/gunner killed in action. This action proved that the Heinkel He 70k planes were not suitable for combat sorties, soon replaced by Heinkel He 111 planes with more credible armament for self defence.

On 08 July the 2/4 Fighter Squadron lost three Fiat Cr.42 planes in bad weather over the Carpathian Mountains. One of the pilots crash-landed but survived, one bailed out and landed with injuries but the third one crashed and killed. Due to these losses, the 2/4 Fighter Squadron was withdrawn soon from the front line.

During the first ten days of the operations, the squadrons flew 145 sorties, dropped 113 tons of bombs. However, crossing the Carpathian Mountains with open cockpit planes with aircrew not trained instrument flight was a risky business.

The airfield at Kolome was secured on 12 July, and the 2/3 Fighter, VII, and X Short-range Reconnaissance Squadrons were relocated there, which made it easier to support the troops and spare the dangerous flights over the mountains.

In mid-July, I and II Short-range Reconnaissance and the 1/3 Fighter Squadrons were deployed to the front line to relived the combat squadrons. The I Squadron had Heinkel He 46 planes commanded by Captain László Bibithy-Horváth, the III Squadron led by Captain József Csegezy had WM-21 aircraft. Captain László Tomor commanded the 1/3 Fighter Squadron, flew with Fiat Cr.42 planes.

The 4th Bomber Regiment was relived in mid-July, it was replaced by the Mixed Bomber Squadron formed from the 3/II, 4/I Bomber Groups, flew with Ju 86K-2 and Ca.135bis bomber planes.

The fighter and short-range reconnaissance squadrons moved forward to Sutyska, their former airfield was taken over by the Mixed Bomber Squadron.

On 11 August six Caproni Ca.135bis bombers attacked targets at Nikolajev, the Hungarian planes were armed with captured Soviet 100 kilogram bombs. The Caproni's led by 1st Lieutenant István Szakonyi scored a direct hit on the railway station and destroyed the bridge over the Bug. 1st Lieutenant Szakonyi plane's, the B.517 was hit by anti-aircraft fire, lost one engine. The Caproni lagged behind the formation, and was attacked by six Soviet I-16 fighters. The Hungarian crew shot down three Soviet fighters and returned to their base. The Caproni's were escorted by six Fiat Cr.42 fighters of the 1/3 Fighter Squadron. The Fiats clashed with Soviet I-16 fighters and shot down five Red Star's planes. On this day five Re 2000 fighters also took off, missed the Soviet fighters, but lost one plane due to ground fire. 1st Lieutenant Gyula Lasztoczy was missing in action with his V.420 plane.

From 7 July to 28 August the Aviation Group flew 555 sorties, dropped just 40 tons of bombs and claimed 27 Soviet planes, and lost four aircraft and six pilots. However, another 41 planes were written off due to accidents.

Lieutenant Colonel Sándor Gyiresy took over the command of the Aviation Group from Lieutenant Colonel Béla Orosz in august of 1941.

On 31 August the Mobile Corps took over the defense of the River Dnieper at about 200 km south of Dnepropetrovsk, while the planes were busy in the airspace over Lozovaya, Izyum, and Kharkov. The Hungarian fighters and bombers supported the troops of the 5th Motorised Rifle Battalion at the Island of Khortytsia in early September. The Hungarian Ju 86K-2 bombers and Fiat Cr.42 fighters bombed and strafed the Soviet forces but could not stop the attackers. The Hungarians withdraw from the Island.

The worsening weather and difficult terrain hindered the activities of both the land forces and air forces, and therefore they had returned to Hungary by mid-December 1941. Although the Mobile Corps and its flying units worked along strategic sidetracks of the Eastern Front, this was a period to gain experience and, according to documents of the general staff they lived up to expectations. During this half-year of wartime experience, the aviation units made 1,454 flights, spent 2,192 hours in the air, dropped 217 tons of bombs, and shot down 30 Soviet planes. At the same time 17 Hungarian officers and airmen died, 4 officers and 2 airmen went missing, and 10 officers and 18 airmen were wounded. The air force lost 25 reconnaissance planes, 14 fighters, 11 bombers, 5 couriers, and 1 transport plane. Most of the aircraft lost due to bad weather and technical problems.

Conclusion

On strategically level the Hungarian involvement during the first phase of the war against the Soviet Union was minimal. Comparing with the rival Romanian Army deployed with two field armies and 325.000 men the Hungarians devoted just five brigades and supporting troops of 89.000 men organized into two army corps controlled by an operational group. The Hungarians are criticized by some historians that deployed insufficient forces in numbers, equipment, and combat readiness.

On the Hungarian side, it was a political decision to commit as few as possible troops on the Eastern Front, to preserve the strength of the Hungarian Army to protect the country and its territorial enlargement won from 1938 to 1941. It was the lessons learned from WW1 for the Hungarians and they paid the price in terms of losing Hungarian territories.

On the other hand, the Hungarian committed their most modern, partially motorized units; the Mobile Corps and the elite mountain jagers and border guard troops of the VIII Corps and the selected units of the Royal Hungarian Air Force. The Hungarians deployed about 80% of their armored vehicles and motorized artillery troops and motor vehicles too.

The role of the Carpathian Operational Group and later the Mobile Corps was to provide links and cover between the attacking German and Romanian forces following the withdrawing Red Army units. The Mobile Corps was mostly performed offensive operations against withdrawing Soviet Forces. The Hungarians pursued the withdrawing Soviet forces or clashed with them in meeting engagements. In the later stage of the campaign, the Hungarians performed River defense operations too.

Hungarian sappers passing an abandoned Soviet BT-7 tank with a white rhombus unit sign painted on the turret. [Fortepan/Kiss]

Abandoned Soviet I-16 fighter plane at the roadside with curious local civilians and a Hungarian soldier. [Fortepan/Kiss]

In another photo of the abandoned Soviet I-16 fighter, the souvenir hunters already stripped the plane and the locals removed the canvas for their use. [Fortepan/Kiss]

The Hungarian mountain jager and a border guard unit opened gateways through the mountainous terrain of the Carpathian for the units of the Mobile Corps. The attacking forces cling on a single supply road among the peaks of the Carpathian Mountain, which was a hazardous decision, but the Soviets were not in the position to utilize it. On the other side, the Hungarian planers were not in knowledge of this fact.

The partially mechanized troops of the Mobile Corps come out of the mountain passes and pursued the withdrawing Soviet Army's units. The Hungarians kept up with the advancing German forces, securing bridgeheads on the River obstacles which frequently crisscrossed the terrain in Ukraine. Later the Mobile Corps was used for sealing cauldrons, covering the German units.

Hungarian soldiers inspecting an abandoned Soviet T-26 light tank in autumn of 1941. The tank looks intact, however, the machine gun was already removed from the turret. [Fortepan/Zagyva]

Hungarian lance corporal posing in the turret of the Soviet T-26 light tank. Behind a tank, quite well-maintained houses are visible, probably somewhere in Eastern Poland. [Fortepan/Zagyva]

Hungarian garrison in a small East-Polish town, the locals were friendly towards the Hungarians. The situation was still peaceful the Hungarians were not armed and wore their field caps irregularly. [Fortepan/Zagyva]

The winter came early in Ukraine, from October the temperature froze and snow fell. Local HQ of the Hungarian occupation forces, the sentry wearing special greatcoats and boots to withstand the winter weather. The officer wears knitted headgear under his field cap. [Fortepan/Székely]

Hungarian pontoon bridge built by the II. Hungarian engineer Battalion over the River South-Bug at Vinica late 1941. [Fortepan/Ungváry]

The Hungarian mobile units advanced on difficult terrain and weather conditions. The geographical features varied from high mountains, through hilly terrain to plains. The operational area was relatively densely populated, causing more suffering to the civilian population, but a better chance to supply the troops with the local acquisition. The weather in June-July was extremely rainy, the Rivers, creeks flooded and the frequent rainfalls turned the dirt roads into slippery quagmires. In August-September, the extreme hotness and lack of water caused problems for men and horses too.

This operation was the baptize of fire of the Hungarian Army since WW1 which was always intended to use against their neighbors to re-conquer and keep the territories lost after WW1. However, in the summer of 1941, it was deployed against the mighty Red Army, which was a fearful opponent even its disintegrated, defeated status. That is what the critics always forget to note. Although by 1941 the Hungarian Army went through significant changes, their weapons, motorization lagged behind the standard weaponry of the major belligerent armies.

The Hungarians utilized the captured Soviet Vorosilovec heavy tracked tractor to haul engineer equipment, materials. Officer candidate sergeant János Bobor, II. Engineer Battalion seats in the cockpit, wearing irregular beret and beard. [Fortepan/Ungváry]

The Hungarian troops passed an abandoned Soviet T-35 medium tank on its way back home. [Fortepan/Hajdú Fedő]

Soviet KV-2 heavy tank left on the roadside during the Soviet retreat. [Fortepan/Hajdú Fedő]

Except for the Yugoslavian campaign, which lasted for less than a week for the Hungarians it was the first real combat operation for the Hungarian Army on large scale. The mechanized warfare was tested first time by the Hungarian commanders, who had no previous experience in how to command, control, and operate mobile forces in combat. The commanders and troops had to learn by casualties how to advance, explore and fight. During the first phase of the operation the scouting was neglected, the Hungarian troops bravely, dashing but headlong attacked the superior Soviet Forces, which led to unnecessary casualties.

The Hungarians fought against superior enemy forces, which withdrawing in an orderly manner, mostly under the pressure of the adjacent German forces to avoid the encirclement. The operational boundaries

he motorized elements of the Mobile Corps drove back from Donetsk to Hungary on road. The frozen surface helped the trucks to return. A broken 38M Botond towed by another Botond. [Fortepan/Csorba]

Hungarian 38M Botond trucks returning Hungary through the Carpathian Mountains in December 1941. [War Correspondent Company]

On a gloomy winter day, Ensign Pál Berkó and his fellow soldiers returned to Hungarian, greeted by the local civilians, soldiers, and nurses at a Hungarian Railway Station. [Fortepan/Berkó]

were set by the Germans and they were not always taken into account the actual combat readiness of the Hungarian Mobile Corps.

The Hungarian used composite combat groups consisted of motorized rifles, bicycle battalions reinforced with light artillery batteries, sapper, light tank and reconnaissance companies, platoons. The advancing combat groups were moved on parallel lines ahead, contrary to the Tactical Manuals, without proper reserve forces. The Soviet units could easily counter attack, stop the advancing Hungarian units. The locally superior Soviet forces bitter clashed with the Hungarian troops. The clashes rapidly developed from the out of blue and fluctuated, the frontlines were uncharted and flexible without clear boundaries between the fighting parties.

During the operation, the staff of the Mobile Corps invented a method how to pursue the withdrawing troops. In theory, the two motorized rifle brigades were deployed on different, parallel roads and the cavalry brigade was deployed between them. The brigade commanders created different combat groups a system developed during the short Yugoslavian Campaign to fulfill the given tasks.

The so-called Combat Groups were named after the commander of the group, who was the senior battalion commander or high-ranking staff officer from the Brigade's HQ. The Combat Groups consisted of one-two motorized rifles and one bicycle battalions, reinforced with one to two light howitzer batteries, sappers, light tank platoon, or company. The idea was that these combat groups were already reinforced with those extra troops needed to carry out their tasks. On the other hand, it meant that the brigade commanders had too little to reinforce their troops if needed. For example, the artillery component of a motorized rifle brigade consisted of a light howitzer battalion with three batteries and the light howitzer battery of its bicycle battalion. It was four batteries, if the brigade commander

The 1st Cavalry Brigade was officially welcomed by the governor, Admiral Horthy at Nyíregyháza in 1941. The cavalry units returned earlier than the motorized units. Hussar squadron parades in front of the governor. [War Correspondent Company]

organized just one battle group and the reconnaissance element it already consumed almost half of its artillery. Two batteries were not enough to provide concentrated fire support if it was needed. The anti-aircraft batteries of the brigade had six 36M 40mm Bofors guns, an excellent weapon against air and land targets, they were allocated in pairs or single to support the troops.

The forward echelon of a motorized rifle brigade consisted of the reconnaissance battalion, which was reinforced by a light tank, anti-aircraft cannons, sapper, anti-tank, machine-gun, and traffic control platoons, and one-one light howitzer battery and motorized rifle company. The second echelon consisted of one motorized rifle battalion from the combat group. The third echelon was the main bulk of the brigade. The last one was the rear guard.

The commander's intent in case of contact was to outflank the enemy or attack them frontally by his deployed troops supported by the brigade artillery. According to the regulation the motorized rifles were transported by their all-terrain trucks close to the combat zone, but the precious trucks were left behind in secure places with guards and the first line was approached on foot like the normal infantry. It was similar for the cavalry and bicycle troops too, to leave behind their bicycles and vehicles. Only the reconnaissance and tank troops went into action on their armored vehicles, motorcycles.

Of course, this was the theory; however, the reality was normally more complicated. The withdrawing Soviet troops showed courage, determination, good fighting skills and carried out many ambushes and counterattacks. In some cases the Hungarian troops neglected the

The victory parade was held for the Mobile Corps in Budapest, 1941. The parading 38M Toldi light tank units belonged to the replacement units because tank battalions lost almost all of their vehicles. [War Correspondent Company]

The operation wore down the armored vehicles; most of them needed a factory overhaul. 38M Toldi light tanks repaired at the Automobile Depot of the Army, next to them a Fiat Ansaldo tankette. [Fortepan/Lissák]

proper reconnaissance, running into ambushes, counter-attacks. The officer corps casualties were numerically higher than the enlisted, on the one hand, they led their troops in front, on the other hand, they were the targets of the Soviet snipers.

Due to the inadequate road network, logistical support for the advancing troops was difficult; sometimes fuel and ammunition had to be transported to the mobile troops by aircraft. The troops lacked recovery vehicles and trailers. The maintenance background of the troops was also weak, and the mobilized civilian trucks were in bad condition. Only the 38M Botond trucks could handle the difficult terrain.

These battles highlighted that in general, the Hungarian units had less firepower than their Red Army counterparts. The Hungarians had no submachine guns, machine guns were WW1 models and mortars were fewer than at their opponents. The Hungarian anti-tank guns and anti-tank rifles as well as the turret weapons of the armored cars and light tanks were just suited against the Soviet T-26 and BT light tanks.

The artillery was an elite branch in the Hungarian Army and performed well during the campaign. The brigade's artillery batteries of the Mobile Corps were mostly distributed among the battle groups leaving minimal artillery at the brigade commanders' disposal to deliver concentrated fire strikes. The rapid firing 40mm Hungarian Bofors anti-aircraft cannons were used as multi-functional guns attached one by one to the combat groups.

The armored vehicles of the Mobile Corps consisted of Italian-made 35M Fiat Ansaldo (CV33) tankettes, totally outdated and 38M Toldi light tanks and 39M Csaba armored cars lightly armored and armed, suitable for reconnaissance and liaison roles only. The lack of medium tanks, self-propelled anti-tank, and anti-aircraft guns were a serious deficiency of the deployed troops.

The pride of the Hungarian Army, the Mobile Corps was partially mechanized, equipped with homemade,

After the operation in 1941, the Fiat Ansaldo tankettes were withdrawn from the service, parking in the yard of the Automobile Depot of the Army. The two tankettes on the right have observation cupolas, the twin machine guns already removed. [Fortepan/Lissák]

German, Italian, and Polish trucks, artillery tractors, and motorcycles. However, it was not enough and the troops had to heavily rely on the mobilized civilian trucks, cars, and motorbikes. The home designed and produced 38M Botond all-terrain squad carrier trucks were among the best WW2 military trucks. The Krupp Protze half-squad carrier and anti-tank artillery tractors, Hansa Lloyd half-tracked, Pavesi, and homemade KV-40 tractors were used by the artillery. The Ford and Ford-Marmon trucks were at the supply column of the combat troops. The civilian trucks, in different technical status, concentrated at the brigade, corps-level supply columns.

The Hungarians brought back captured Soviet materials exhibited in Budapest in 1942. The civilians curiously inspect the T-20 Komsomolec artillery tractor. [Fortepan/Angyalföld]

War materials captured on the Eastern front exhibited in Budapest, on the right side are armored vehicles, Polish R-35, T-60, BT-7 tanks, Polish TK tankette. The Polish material arrived in late September 1939 in Hungary. [P. Mujzer]

Captured artillery pieces, 85mm anti-aircraft gun, 76mm regimental and mountain guns, 122mm howitzer visible on the photo. [P. Mujzer]

The Hungarian equipment and uniforms based on the K. und K. Armee articles relatively performed well. The signal units operated Hungarian made radios and field telephones with landlines, but the dispatch riders still were key assets of the communications.

The supplies of the troops were difficult; the lines of communications were long and weak. The campaign was fought as coalition warfare, where the axis forces fixed the terms and conditions of the warfighting as well as the supply of the troops. However, the German logistic supply centers were situated far behind the operational area and it was the responsibility of the Hungarians to pick up and deliver the goods to the troops. The captured Soviet logistic stocks helped and eased the critical logistic shortfalls. Nevertheless, the fuel shortage was a constant problem and negatively influenced the mobility of the Mobile Corps.

The war on the Eastern Front fought from the beginning with an unspoken cruelty by both sides.

During the early stage of the operation the Hungarians were welcomed by the local Polish and Ukrainian population as liberators. Due to the cruelty of the Soviet regime and the NKVD the locals were very supportive to the advancing troops, helping, guiding and informing about the whereabouts of the Red Army troops. Later, on the territories of the Soviet State, the attitude of the population were more hostily and the Soviet State organised partisan activities were more common. Due to the quick advance of the Axis forces and the disintegrated command and control of the Red Army, huge number of Soviet soldiers in groups or individually wandered behind the Axis lines. There were a huge gap between the dashing Axis armoured/mechanised forces and the infantry units mopping up and consolidate the captured territories. On the no-man land withdrawing Soviet soldiers, military aged civilians, deserters and armed local bands emerged from out of blue targeting smaller Axis units, supply columns. It was difficulte to to judge who was combatant and civilian protected by rule of wars and who was unlawful combatant without the protection of the law.

From the beginning of the operation the Hungarians met with the cruel and unusulla warfare of the Soviet Army. Hungarian troops often found their missing soldiers tortured, mutilated and murdered by the Red soldiers. The local population showed the Hungarians the graves of the unlawfully executed Hungarian soldiers. The troops were also frequently ambushed by Soviet forces or partisans wearing Hungarian uniforms, ponchos or civilian cloths hiding their true entities.

This acts quickly brutalised the Hungarian's attitudes towards their enemies as well as towards the civilian population.

The Hungarian acted and sometimes overreacted to the cruel behaviour of the Red Army and the possible treath of partisans. The behaviour of the Hungarian Army on the Eastern Front shaped by the memoires and the practicy performed by the k. und k. Armee during the WW1. The commanding officers of the troops served and indoctrinated during the WW1 too. During the Great War the spyes, souscpicious civilians were heavy handed by the Austro-Hungarian Army which left a mark on the Hungarian Army too. According to the law of war as it was interpretated by the Hungarian troops, the Soveit soldiers captured in Hungarian uniform or civil cloth but armed meant execution on the spot. Souspicious, military aged civilians wandering in combat zone was also in danger if captured by Hungarians. The attitudes of the Hungarians were severly influenced by their loses, nervousnes

During the river defence at Dniepr, the infiltrating civilian clothed Soviet soldiers, NKDV agents mixing with the population were a constant danger for the Hungarians. The villages in the combat zone were screened, the non locals, either refugees or partisans were separated from the population and interned. To stop the partisan activities hostages were selected and executed in case of guerrilla activities. These draconian measures just anticipated the horror of partisan war raged on the Eastern Front from late 1941 until 1944.

The deployed Hungarian units had 89505 men and lost 4991 men, a very moderate 5,5% casualty, especially comparing with the German and Romanian troops not even speak about the Soviet casualties. On the other hand, the material losses were significant. The armored units of the Mobile Corps lost all of its Italian-made tankettes, 90% of the 39M armored cars and 80% of the 38M light tanks were written off. However, the knocked out or damaged light tanks and armored cars were collected and transported back to Hungary for repair. The Hungarians also lost 28 different guns and howitzers, more than 50 aircraft, and 1200 trucks.

However, the tank versus tank clashes was rarer between the Soviet and Hungarian forces, in case of a suspected tank attack, the Hungarians deployed their 37mm anti-tank guns and 40mm Bofors guns, which could knock out the Soviet light tanks.

According to the records the Mobile Corps knocked out 21 tanks, captured 34 tanks, 25 tracked artillery tractors, and 370 trucks. The Hungarians also seized 66 filed, anti-aircraft guns and 15 anti-tank guns. The Soviets also left behind 10.000-liter fuel, logistic dumps with food, ammunition, and equipment too. The Hungarian troops also captured, cannibalized abandoned Soviet war materials to replace their losses. The officers and troops zealously collected and brought back war trophies too.

Bibliography

A m. kir. Fegyveres erők képeskrónikája (1919-1945), Vitézi Szék, 1977

Adonyi-Náredny Ferenc – Nagy Kálmán: Magyar huszárok a II. Világháborúban, HHA, 1990

Babucs Zoltán: Jászsági honvédek a II. világháborúban, I. A jászberényi harckocsi zászlóalj története a II. világháborúban, 2000

Babucs Zoltán – Maruzs Roland: „Jász vitézek rajta, előre!" A jászberényi kerékpáros és harckocsizó zászlóalj története 1920-1944, Puedlo

Balla Tibor – Csikány Tamás – Gulyás Géza – Horváth Csaba – Kovács Vilmos: A magyar tüzérség 100 éve, 1913-2013, Zrínyi 2014

Dr. Barczy Zoltán – Sárhidai Gyula : A Boforstól a Doráig, A magyar légvédelmi tüzérség 1914 – 1945, Petit Real, 2008

Bene János: Nyíregyházi katonaság a II. világháborúban 1938-1945, Józsa András Múzeum 2016

Bíró Ádám – Éder Miklós – Sárhidai Gyula: A magyar királyi honvédség külföldi gyártású páncélos harcjárművei 1920- 1945, Petit Real, 2006

Bíró Ádám – Éder Miklós – Sárhidai Gyula: A magyar királyi honvédség hazai gyártású páncélos harcjárművei 1920- 1945, Petit Real, 2012

Bonhardt Attila – Sárhidai Gyula – Winkler Róbert: A magyar királyi honvédség fegyverzete 1919-45 part 1, Zrínyi, 1992

Bús János- Szabó Péter: Béke poraikra, VARIETAS'93, 1999

Bús János- Szabó Péter: Béke poraikra II.. VARIETAS'93, 2001

Dálnoki Veress Lajos: Magyarország honvédelme a II. világháború előtt és alatt (1920-1945), München, 1974

Dombrády Loránd-Tóth Lajos: Magyar Királyi Honvédség 1919 45, Zrínyi, 1987

Dombrády Loránd: A magyar gazdaság és a hadfelszerelés, 1938/44, Akadémia, 1981

Csima János: Források a Magyar Honvédség II. világháborús történetének tanulmányozásához, Zrínyi, 1961

Gosztonyi Péter. A Magyar Honvédség a II. világháborúban, Európa, 1992

Görgey Vince: Páncélosok előre!, Stádium, 1942

Illésfalvi Péter – Kovács Vilmos – Maruzs Roland: Vitézségért, HK Hermanos, 2011

Magyarország a II. világháborúban, Enciklopédia, PETIT REAL, 1997

Maruzs Roland: Középkereszt, tisztikereszt, lovagkereszt, Zrínyi, 2013

Mányi Pál: Magyar páncélosokkal a hadak útján 1941-1944, Magánkiadás 2000

M. Szabó Miklós: A Magyar királyi honvéd légierő a 2. világháborúban, Zrínyi Kiadó 1987

Szabó Péter – Számvéber Norbert: A keleti hadszíntér és Magyarország 1941- 1943, Puedlo

Rada Tibor: A magyar királyi honvéd Ludovika Akadémia és testvérintézetek összefoglaló története 1930-1945, GÁLOS NYOMDÁSZ Bt, 1998

Rainer M. János: Századosok, Osiris Kiadó, 2018

Stark Tamás: Hadak Útján, Corvina, 1991

Sőregi Zoltán – Végső István: Gyorsan, bátran, hűséggel, A m. kir. „Balogh Ádám" 15. honvéd kerékpáros zászlóalj története, Timp Kiadó 2009

Sőregi Zoltán: Katonák kerékpáron, A magyar királyi honvédség kerékpáros tisztjeinek adattára 1920-1945, Magánkiadás 2014

Ungváry Krisztián: A magyar honvédség a második világháborúban, Osiris, 2005

Zachár Sándor: Katonai Zseb-lexikon, 1939

Articles

ZMKA Akadémiai Közlemények:

Dr. Lengyel Ferencz: M. kir. I. Gyors Hadtest hadműveletei a Szu elleni háborúban 1941 július 9. november 15., 1994/204

Hadtörténeti Közlemények:

Tóth Lajos: A Gyorshadtest a Szovjetunióban, HK 1966/2

Dombrándy Loránd: A horthysta katonai vezetés erőfeszítései a páncélos fegyvernem megteremtésére, HK 1969/2, 1970/4

Haditechnikai Szemle:

Bíró Ádám: The AC-II, 39M Csaba páncélgépkocsik, 1992/3

Bíró Ádám: A magyar páncélos fegyvernem kezdetei, 2. rész, a FIAT Ansaldo 35M, 1993/3

Fröhlich Dávid: A magyar sereglovasság tüzérségi eszközei és tüzér szervezeti elemei, 2013/6

Dr. Klemensits Péter: A Magyar páncélos erők a Szovjetunió elleni hadműveletekben – a Toldi könnyű harckocsi I. rész, 2016/1

Dr. Klemensits Péter: A Magyar páncélos erők a Szovjetunió elleni hadműveletekben – a Toldi könnyű harckocsi II. rész, 2016/2

Dr. Mujzer Péter: A magyar páncélos fegyvernem kezdetei I. rész, 2016/1

Dr. Mujzer Péter: A magyar páncélos fegyvernem szervezeti és fegyverzeti fejlesztése 1938-1942 I. rész, 2016/2

Dr. Mujzer Péter:A Magyar Királyi Honvédség páncélos szervezeteinek részvétele a Szovjetunió elleni hadműveletekben 1941-ben, 2017/3

Somkutas Róbert: A Magyar Királyi Honvédség páncélozott eszközökkel felszerelt felderítő Chopatai I. rész, 2016/1

Somkutas Róbert: A Magyar Királyi Honvédség páncélozott eszközökkel felszerelt felderítő Chopatai II. rész, 2016/2

Somkutas Róbert: A Magyar Királyi Honvédség páncélozott eszközökkel felszerelt felderítő Chopatai III. rész, 2016/3

Somkutas Róbert: A Magyar Királyi Honvédség páncélozott eszközökkel felszerelt felderítő Chopatai IV. rész, 2016/4

Somkutas Róbert: A Magyar Királyi Honvédség páncélozott eszközökkel felszerelt felderítő Chopatai V. rész, 2016/5

Somkutas Róbert: A Magyar Királyi Honvédség páncélozott eszközökkel felszerelt felderítő Chopatai VI. rész, 2016/6

Somkutas Róbert: A Magyar Királyi Honvédség páncélozott eszközökkel felszerelt felderítő Chopatai VII. rész, 2017/2

Somkutas Róbert: A Magyar Királyi Honvédség páncélozott eszközökkel felszerelt felderítő Chopatai VIII. rész, 2017/3

Somkutas Róbert: A Magyar Királyi Honvédség páncélozott eszközökkel felszerelt felderítő Chopatai IX. rész, 2017/4

Somkutas Róbert: A Magyar Királyi Honvédség páncélozott eszközökkel felszerelt felderítő Chopatai X. rész, 2017/5

Somkutas Róbert: A Magyar Királyi Honvédség páncélozott eszközökkel felszerelt felderítő Chopatai XI. rész, 2017/6

Katona Újság

Simon Tamás: Az 1. gépkocsizó dandár a nyikolajevi csatában, 2013/4.

Militaria Modell:

Éder Miklós: Magyar páncélos járművek alakulat jelzései, 1. rész, 1991 / 1

Éder Miklós: Magyar páncélos járművek alakulat jelzései, 2. rész, 1991/2

Éder Miklós: 38M Toldi könnyűharckocsi, 1991/3

Éder Miklós: 39M Csaba páncélgépkocsi, 1992/1

Éder Miklós: LK-II harckocsi a Magyar Honvédségnél, 1992/2

Éder Miklós: Magyar páncélos Chopatok bőrruházata, 1992/4

Éder Miklós: Magyar páncélosok hadi jelzése, 1917-1945, 1992/6

Pro Modell

Mujzer Péter: A magyar királyi honvédség páncélos Chopatainak jelzésrendszere, 2003/1-3

Foreign Books

Max Axworthy: Third Axis Fourth Ally, Arms and Armour, 1995

Dr Tamás Baczoni – Dr László Tóth: Hungarian Army Uniforms 1939 – 1945, HUNIFORM 2010

Csaba Becze: Magyar steel, Mashroom Publication, 2006

Dénes Bernád, Charles K. Kliment: Magyar Warriors, The history of the Royal Hungarian Armed Forces 1919-1945, volumen 1, Helion Publication, 2015

Dénes Bernád, Charles K. Kliment: Magyar Warriors, The history of the Royal Hungarian Armed Forces 1919-1945, volumen 2, Helion Publication, 2017

Ruppert Butler: Hitler's Jackals, Leo Cooper, 1998

Patrick Cloutier: Three Kings: Axis Royal Armies on the Russian Front 1941, 2014
Terry J. Gander: The 40mm Bofors Gun, 1986 Patrick Stephens Ltd.
Peter Gosztonyi: Deutschlands waffengefahrten an de rost front 1941-1941, Motorbuch Verlag, 1981
George Forty: World War Two AFVs, Osprey, 1998
George Forty: World War Two Tanks, Osprey, 1996
George Forty: World War Two Tanks, Osprey, 1995
Jeffry Fowler: Axis Cavalry in World War II, Osprey, 2001
Hakan Gustavsson – Ludovico Slongo: Fiat CR.42 Aces of World War 2, Osprey 2009
Werner Haupt: Army Group South, Schiffer, 1998
Charles Kliment- Vladimir Francev: Czechoslovakian AFVs 1918-1948, Schiffer, 1997
Charles Kliment – Bretislav Nakláda: Germany's First Ally, Schiffer 1997
Janusz Ledwoch: Eastern Front 1941-45, Militaria, 1995
Victor Madej: South-Eastern Europe Axis Armies Handbook, Game Marketing Company, 1982
Military Intelligence Division: Order of Battle and Handbook of the Hungarian Armed Forces, 1944 US War Dep. (restricted)
Eduardo Gil Martinez: Fuerzas Acorazadas Húngaras 1939-43, Almena 2017
Péter Mujzer: Hungarian Mobile Forces 1920-45, Bayside Books, 2000
Péter Mujzer: Huns on Wheels, Hungarian Mobile Forces in WWII, Armoured, Cavalry, Bicycle Troops, Motorised Rifle, Mujzer and Partners Ltd., 2015
Péter Mujzer: Hungarian Armoured Forces in WWII, KAGERO Books, PHOTOSNIPER 26., 2017
Péter Mujzer: Operational history of the Hungarian Armoured Troops in WWII, KAGERO Books, PHOTOSNIPER 28., 2018
Péter Mujzer: 38M Toldi light tank, KAGERO Books, PHOTOSNIPER 31., 2021
Leo Niehorster: The Royal Hungarian Army 1920-45, Bayside Books, 1998
Janusz Pielkalkiewicz: The Cavalry 1939-45, Macdonald, 1986
Georg Punka: Hungarian air force in WW2, Squadron Signal Publication
Janusz Pielkalkiewicz: Tank War 1939-1945, Guild Publishing, 1986
Gyula Sárhidai-György Punka.Viktor Kozlik: Hungarian Eagles, Hikoki Books 1995
Nigel Thomas- László Pál Szabó: The Royal Hungarian Army in World War II, Ospery, 2008
Anthony Tucker-Jones: Armored warfare and Hitler's allies 1941-1945, Pen&Sword, 2013
Steven Zaloga: Armored trains, Osprey, 2008
Steven Zaloga- James Grandsen: The Eastern Front, Arms and Armour, 1983
Steven Zaloga: Tanks of Hitler's eastern allies 1941-45, Osprey, 2013
Charles Winchester: Ostfront, Hitler's war on Russia 1941-1945, Osprey, 1998

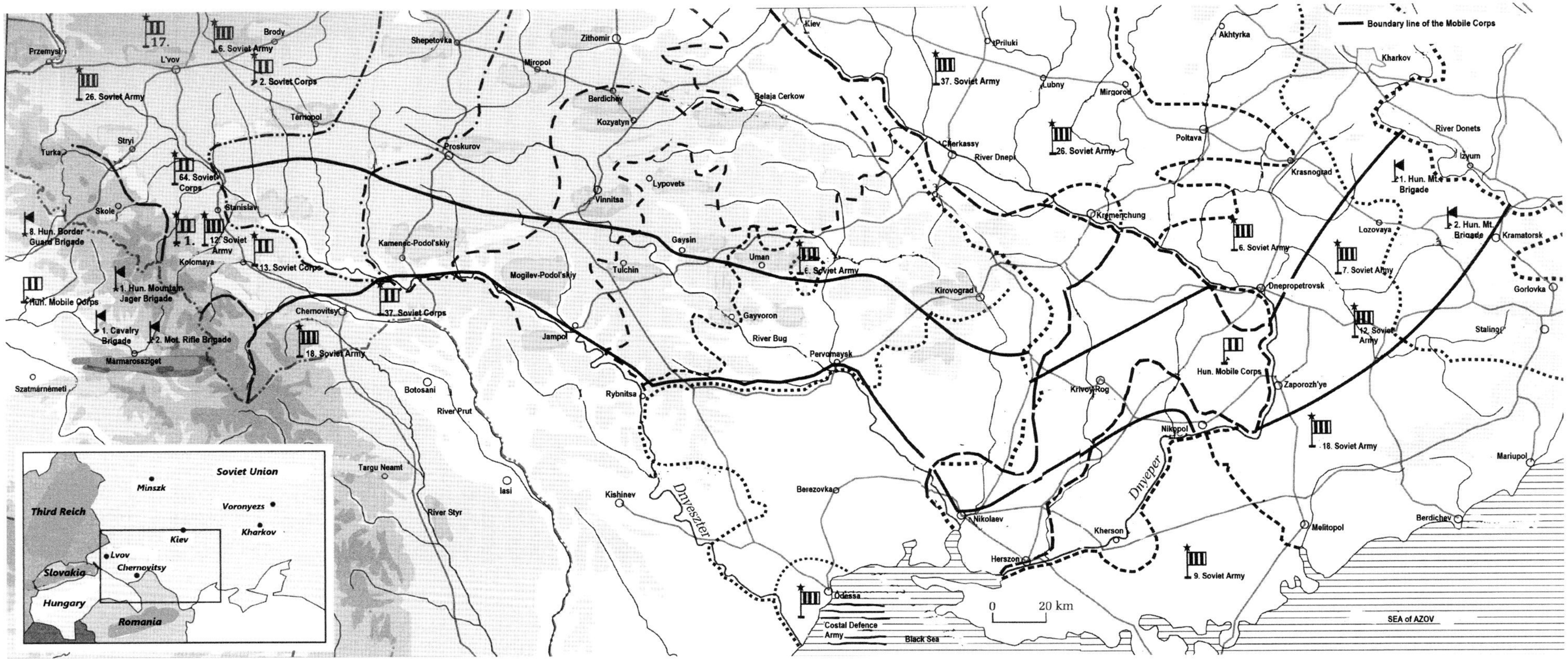

Overview map shows the operational area of the Hungarian Mobile Corps from June to November 1941. The dotted lines represent the timing sequences of the advance.

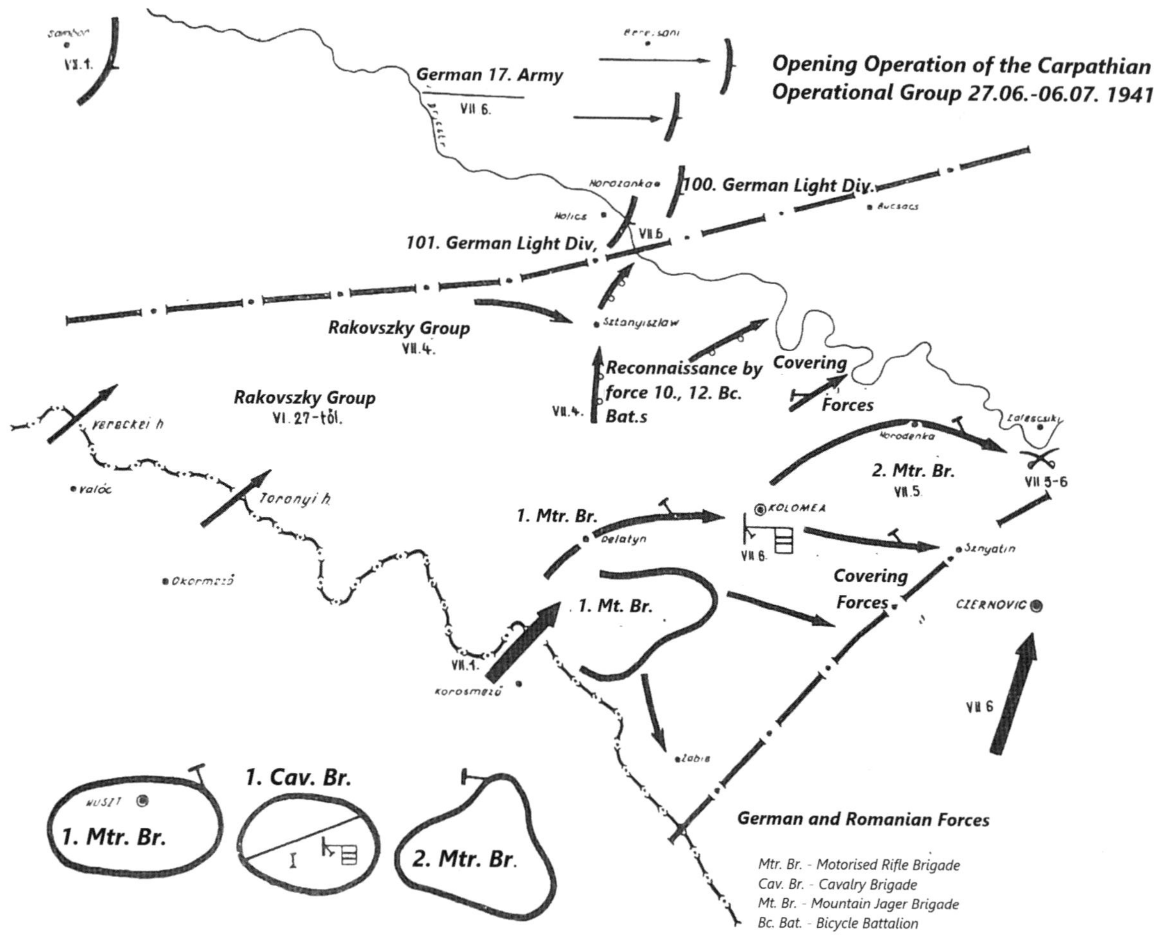

Opening Operation of the Carpathian Operational Group from 27 June to 07 July 1941. The mountain, border guard and bicycle units opened the road for the Mobile Corps to break out of the Carpathian Mountains.

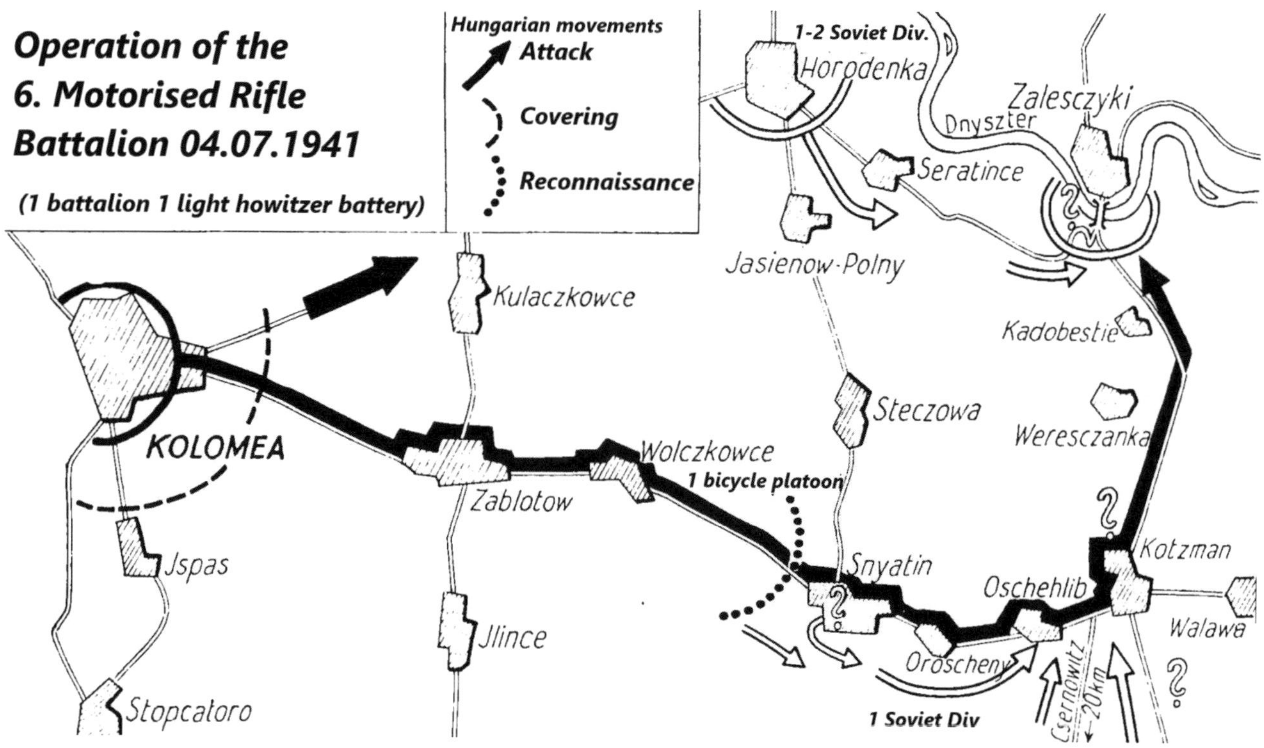

Operation of the 6th Motorised rifle Battalion on 04. July 1941, was a typical clash between the withdrawing, but superior Soviet forces and the reinforced Hungarian motorised rifle battalion. The Hungarians tried to capture the bridges intact.

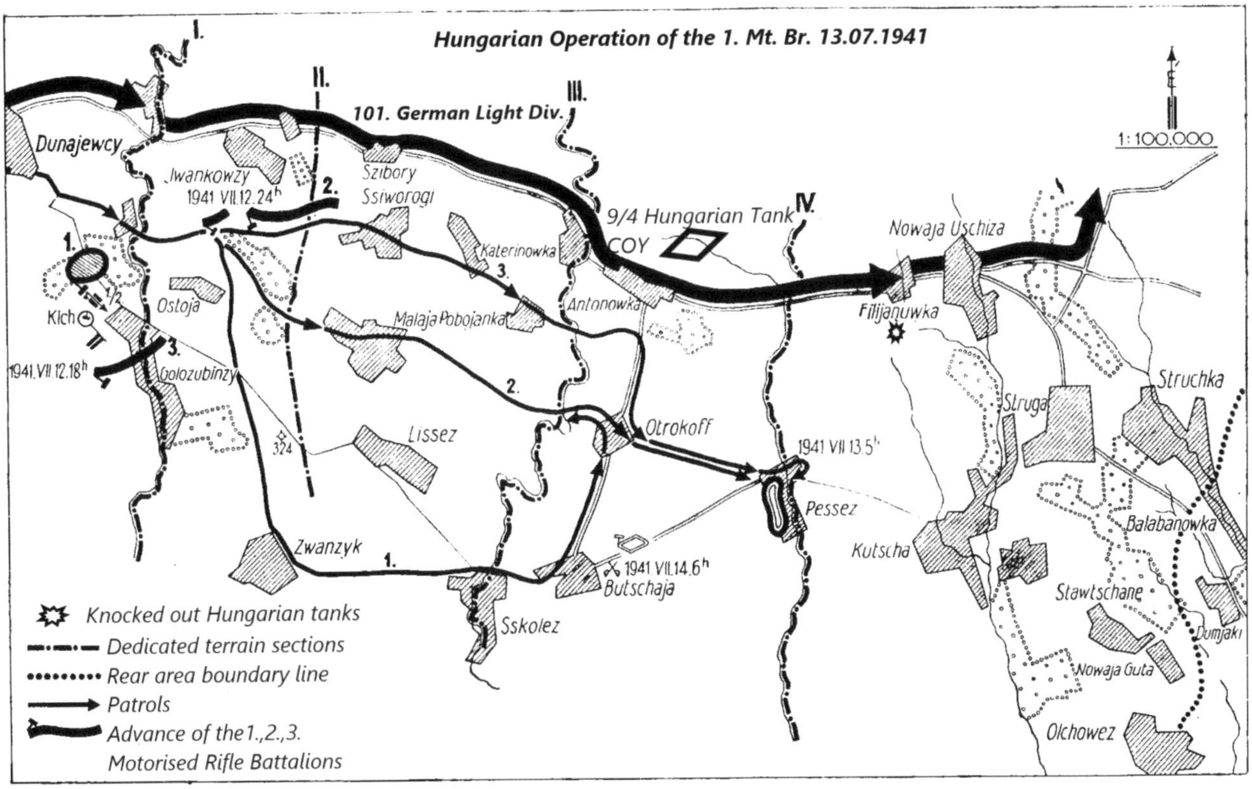

Operation of the 1st Motorised Rifle Brigade, especially its 9th Light Tank Battalion on 13 July 1941 at Filjanovka, in support of the 101st German Light/Jager Division, where the Hungarian tanks suffered serious loses.

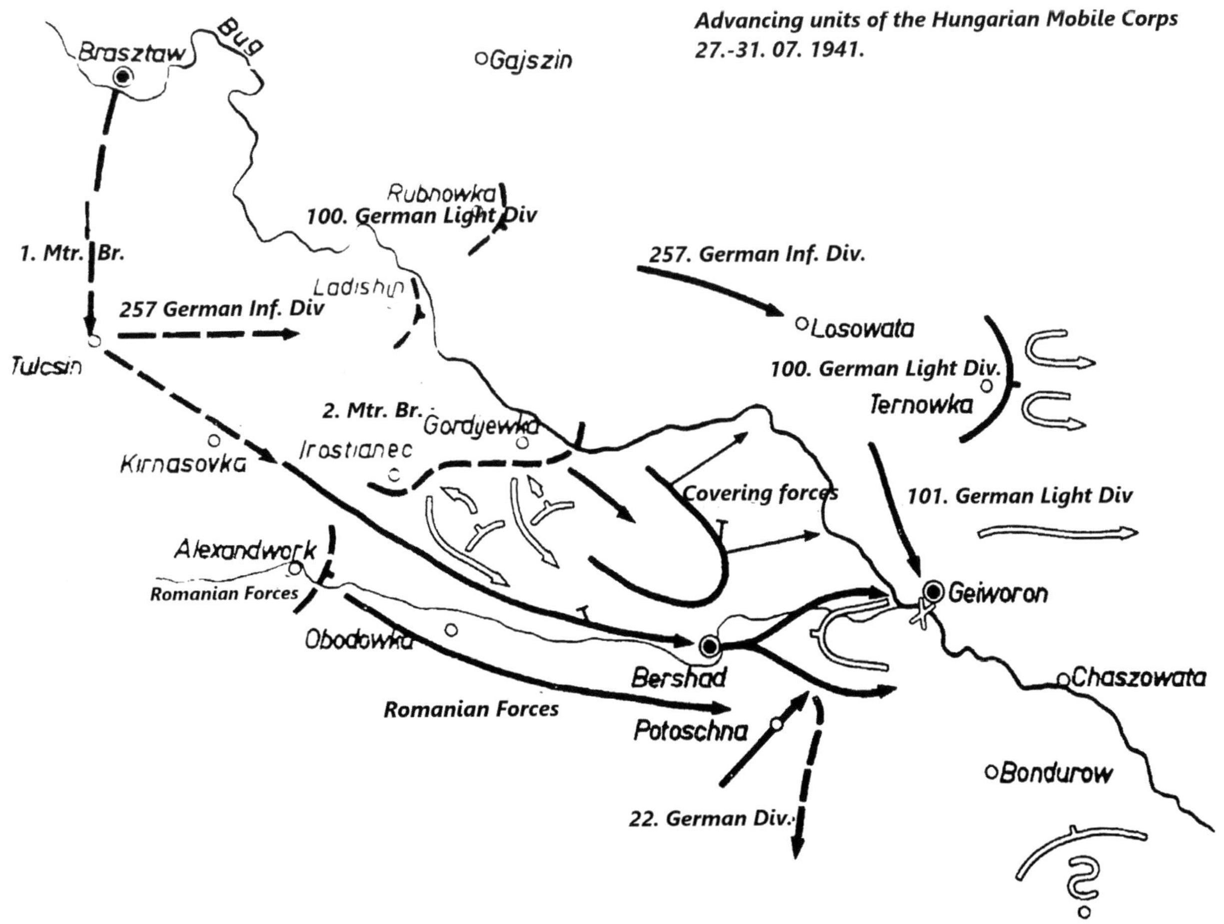

Hungarian Mobile Corps advanced from 27 to 31 July towards River Bug. During this period the units of the 2nd Motorised Rifle and the 1st Cavalry Brigades fought serious battles with strong Soviet forces, especially around Gordievka.

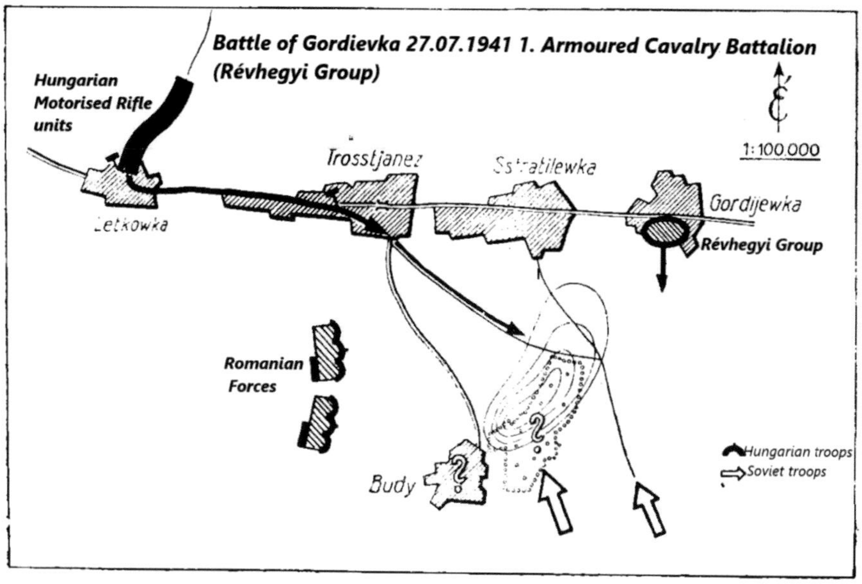

First the tankette companies of the 1st Armoured Cavalry Battalion of the Révhegyi Group was deployed on 27 July from Gordievka to stop the counterattacking Soviet forces. This battle ended the operational career of the FIAT Ansaldo tankettes.

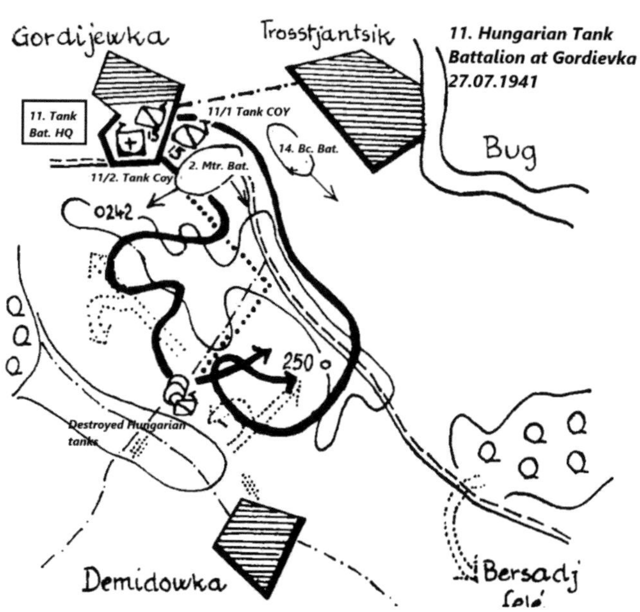

The 11th Light Tank Battalion was ordered to charge on the afternoon of 27 July from Gordievka to stop the Soviet Forces, losing half of its Toldi tanks during the combat. The medical officer of the battalion made this map.

On 06 August 1941, a Hungarian armoured car platoon with two 39M Csaba armoured cars stopped and annihilated a Soviet unit tried to break trough at Golovanevsk.

▼

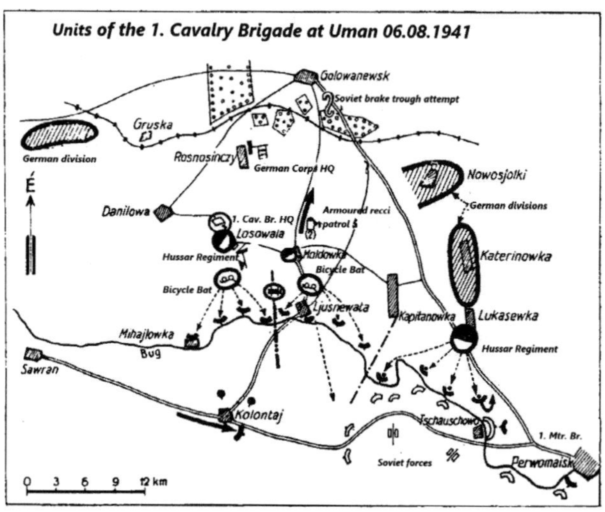

The units of the Hungarian 1st Cavalry Brigade deployed around Uman to stop the breaking trough attempts of the Soviet troops. Most of the units covered the River Bug, linked together with the units of the 1st Motorised rifle Brigade at Pervomajsk.

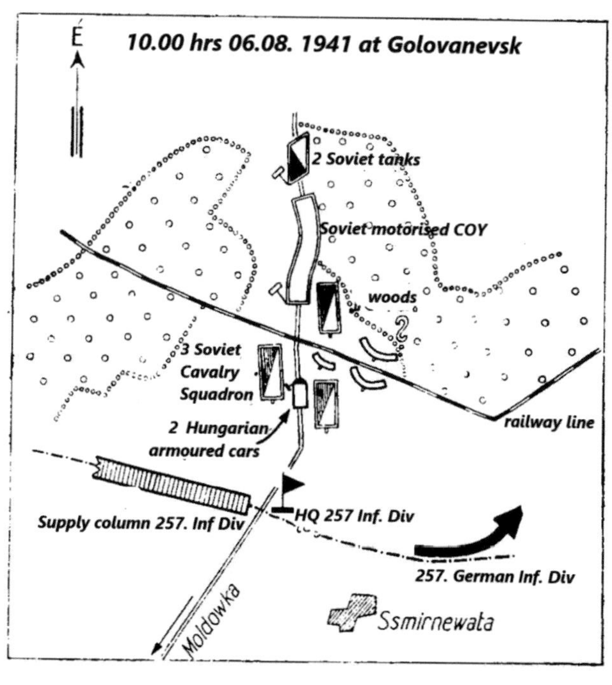

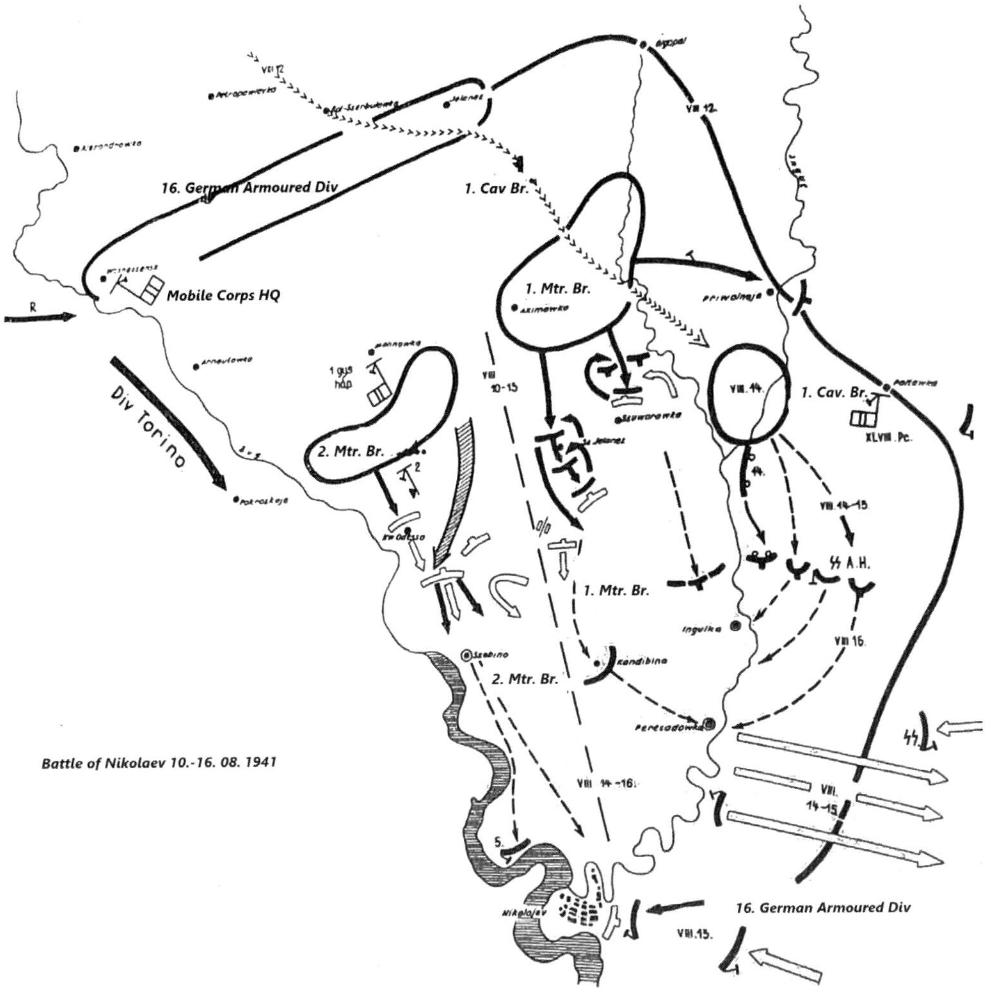

The Hungarian Mobile Corps took part in the battle of Nikolaev from 10 to 16 August 1941. The Hussar regiments of the 1st Cavalry Brigade played active role during the operation.

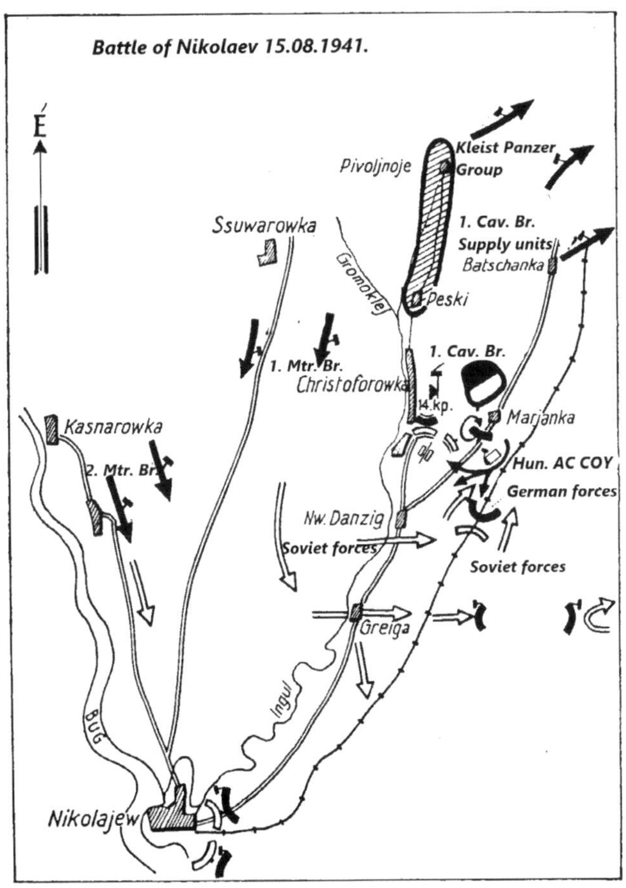

On 15 August at Nowaja Danzig the Hungarian cavalry performed the last cavalry charge of the Hungarian Army.

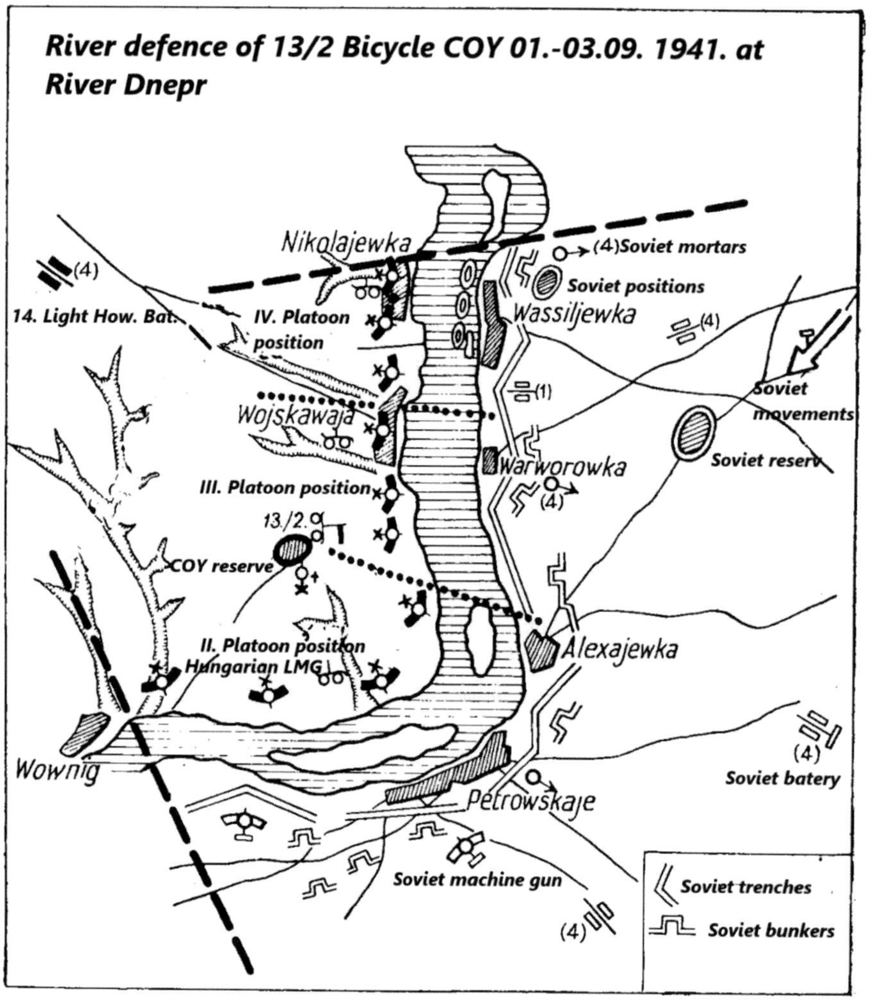

The Hungarian Mobile Corps performed river defence at Dnepr from September to mid October. The Hungarian troops had a weak defence line, like the 13/2 Bicycle Company which had just 11 light machineguns and one anti-tank rifle to counter the superior fire power of the Soviet units.

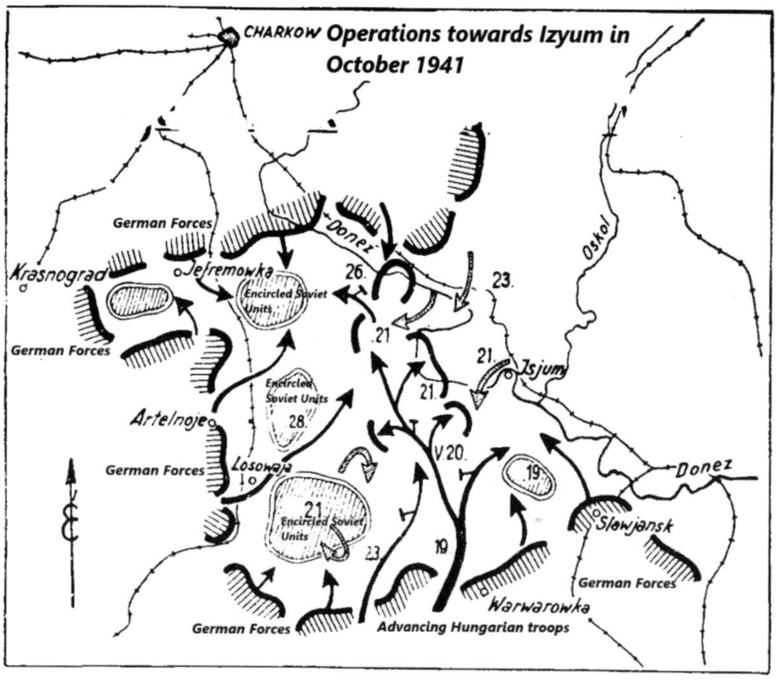

During the final stage of their operation the Mobile Corps reduced to two weak motorised rifle brigades advancing towards Izyum. The rainy and cold weather seriously hampered the operation.

WE RECOMMEND

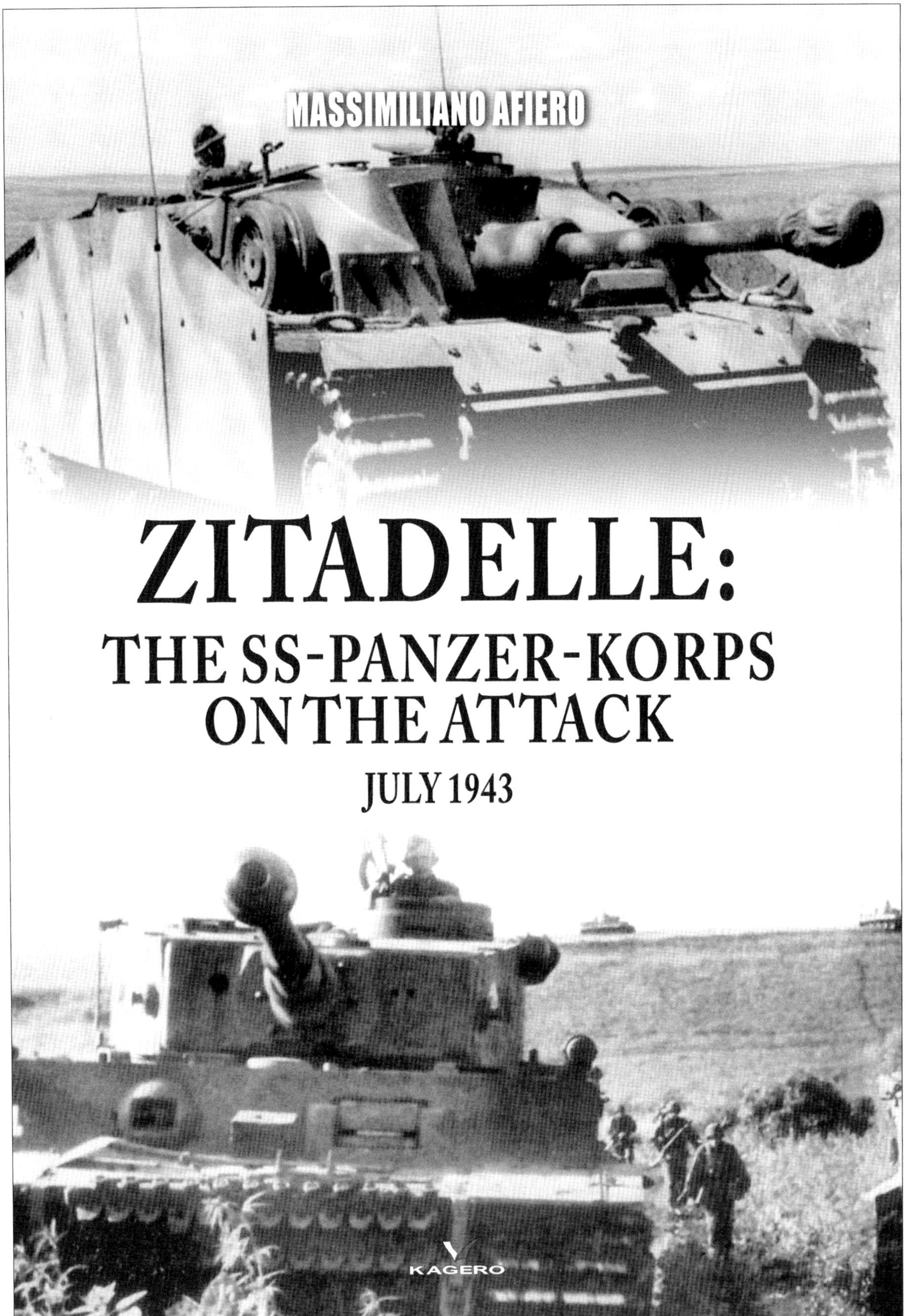

SHOP.KAGERO.PL

WE RECOMMEND

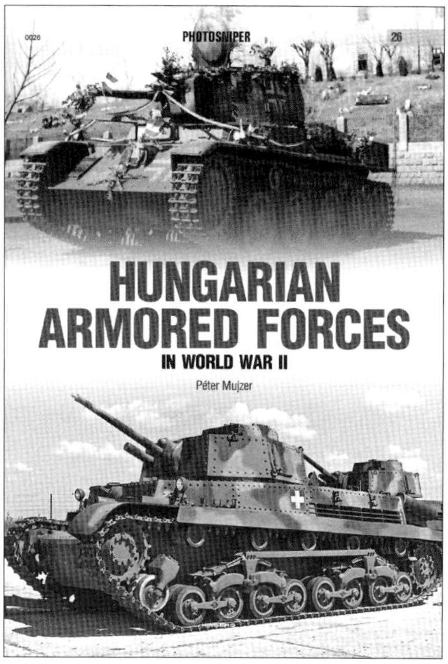

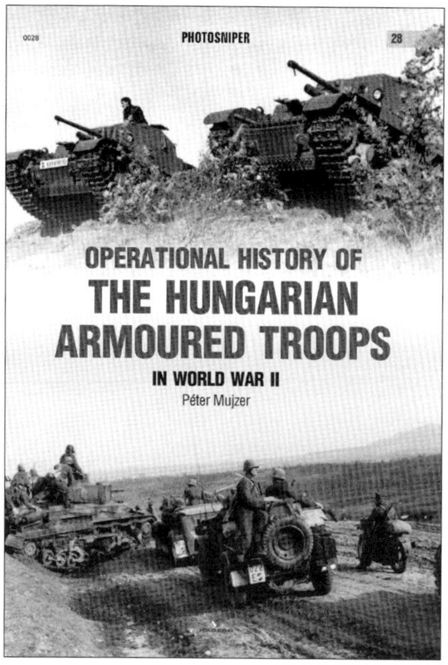

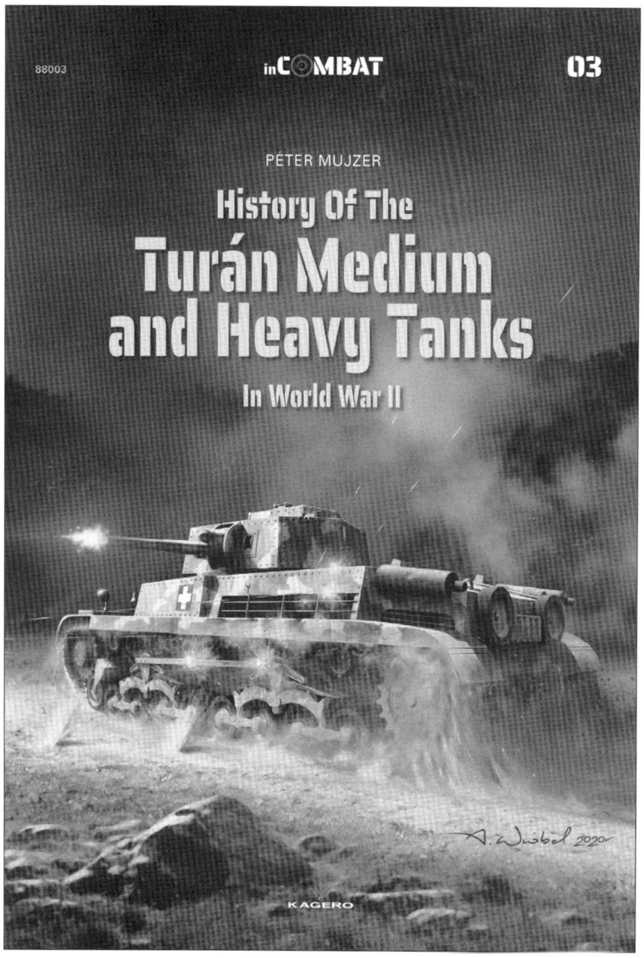

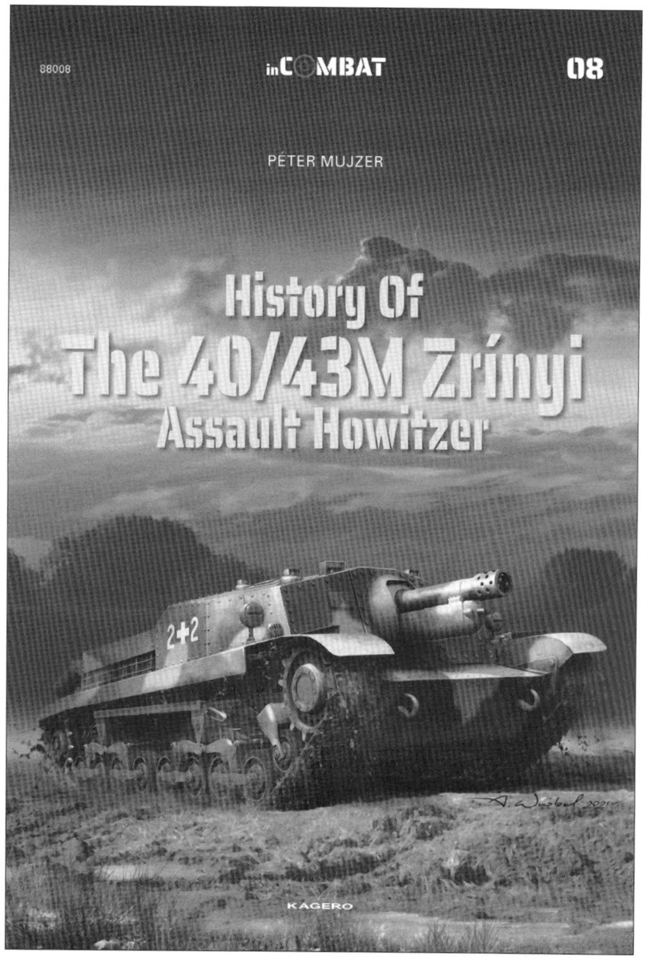

SHOP.KAGERO.PL

Painted by Arkadiusz Wróbel

38M Toldi light tank belonged to the 9th Tank Battalion during the summer of 1941. The light tank still wears the old unit sign of the 1st Light Tank Company of the 1st Armoured Cavalry Battalion, but that time it was relocated to the 9th Tank Battalion.

38M Toldi light tank with standard tree colour camouflage, octagonal military insignia and Mechanised Branch Sign painted on the turret, belonged to the 11th Tank Battalion in the summer of 1941.

39M Csaba armoured car belonged to the 1st Reconnaissance Battalion during the operation in Ukraine in 1941. The armoured car has three colour camouflage with octagonal military insignia painted on the hull.

Painted by Arkadiusz Wróbel

39M Csaba armoured car belonged to the 2nd Reconnaissance Battalion wearing the circular military insignia, only used by the 2nd Reconnaissance Battalion during the campaign.

Painted by Deák Tamás

35M Fiat Ansaldo tankette of the 1st Armoured Cavalry Battalion, with large scale octagonal military insignia, the vehicle has the Hungarian built observation cupola for platoon and company commanders.

35M Fiat Ansaldo tankett of the 1st Armoured Cavalry Battalion. The white skull with lightning original was the unit sign of the tankette platoon of the 14th Bicycle Battalion. The battalion and company signs painted on all sides of the vehicle.

Painted by Sławomir Zajączkowski

The Hungarians got some Heinkel He 111P-2/P-4 long-range reconnaissance version of the Heinkel He 111 bomber planes. This plane stationed at the airfield of Pécs has the B.702 code which was changed to F. soon. The Hungarian Heinkel planes made long-range sorties over Ukraine in 1941.

Fiat Cr.42 fighter biplane belonged to the 2/4 Fighter Squadron still wearing the operational markings of the Yugoslavian Campaign. The 2/4 Fighter Squadron took part in the home defence during the summer of 1941.

Painted by Alessandro Cordasco, Camillo Cordasco